One Plus One Makes THREE

A Resilient Woman, an Army
of Angels, and a Stubborn Man.
What Could Go Wrong?

Melissa Schaff

One Plus One Makes Three

Transcendent Publishing
PO Box 66202
St. Pete Beach, FL 33736

ISBN: 978-1-7332773-8-9

Disclaimer: This book is a memoir. It reflects the author's present recollections of experiences over time. Some names and characteristics have been changed, some events have been compressed, and some dialogue has been recreated.

Printed in the United States of America.

The Guys (aka guardian angels, angels or guides): A conglomerate of angels dedicated to helping you grow spiritually. Their information is spiritually-based but they can also answer questions about your physical experiences. They are formal but occasionally attempt levity. Their knowledge is vast but limited; they are *not* omnipotent.

INTRODUCTION

Dear Reader -

Writing has always been cathartic for me. Long before the blog world came into being, I used journaling as a tool to help heal my pain. I never wanted to write a book; I even fought against the idea. Angels, family members, acquaintances (living and deceased) and even strangers told me I needed to do so. It wasn't until one of my budding intuitive students said, "All I've heard since class started was 'book, book, book,'" that I realized I was postponing the inevitable.

Oh, for pity's sake, everyone! I'll write the damn book(s)!

This is the first. It's a memoir about fated events: how I grudgingly left Corporate America; how I was led to – and found my passion through – Reiki, and how my intuition and connection with the angels grew, despite living in the conservative Midwest.

It's also a love story. You'll discover how I finally found my soulmate, only to face seemingly insurmountable obstacles. There's raw, real-life dialogue, inspirational angelic communication and intuitive predictions. Through it all, you will find that out of something "bad," something good will come. Each and every time.

If sharing my personal – and sometimes quite painful - experiences can help one person (maybe, you?) heal, then I will write. If it helps more, all the better.

I am a Writer. I am an Intuitive. I am a Healer. I am a Teacher.

To my most precious Sass Pants;
May you understand the miracle you truly are.

CHAPTER 1

I instantly disliked Ben. His quiet manner, subdued intelligence, and Midwestern work ethic spelled trouble for me professionally. Sure enough, within weeks of his hire, Ben gained management's attention and was promoted to a job that I coveted.

Hoping he would fail and wanting to revel in it, I covertly watched him. What I saw, much to my dismay, was that regardless of stature or education, he treated others with fairness. Begrudgingly, I started to admire and respect him. Then, after attending a few work and social events, and after he had received yet another promotion, we began dating.

It was then I learned, but refused to see, that this golden boy had an Achille's heel: alcohol.

Like most couples, we would stay home some nights and socialize on others. For Ben, socializing meant drinking, often to excess. When after more than a year of dating he asked me to marry him, I assumed he would let go of his partying lifestyle and focus on us; we would be two happily married peas in a pod.

But Ben didn't let it go; he didn't even show any signs of slowing down. I lost count of the times I waited for him like a faithful dog while he was out golfing or playing poker. My reward: he would come home late and, without so much as a glance in my direction, fall drunkenly into our bed.

As I grew increasingly angry, disillusioned and tired of my husband's unilateral choices, discussions turned into arguments and, sometimes, into screaming matches. It wasn't long until resentment took hold. And like a noxious weed, if it wasn't dealt with immediately, it would grow, spread and eventually take over everything. It is a killer of relationships.

I began journaling as a way of venting and keeping track of my growing feelings of disgust and despair, and within three months had a tangible record of our declining marriage. This included documentation of several drunken verbal assaults which were usually followed by sober apologies and promises he couldn't keep.

Though I tried not to believe what Ben said to me during those rages, they often found their mark and took a toll on my self-esteem. When I finally admitted to myself that I was depressed, instead of seeking a mental health professional or anti-depressants, my solution was to drink alcohol. Based on my childhood, this was how I knew to cope.

The worst part was that except for a few close friends no one knew what I was going through. In public, Ben and I maintained the appearance of the perfect mates – attentive, respectful and supportive of each other. But behind closed doors, I felt isolated and cried more often than not.

Our one-year anniversary came and went, then our second and third. Somewhere along the way we tried counseling, but Ben didn't think much of it. On what would be our last session, he told the counselor I was the cause of his drinking. Like any good therapist, she was not having any of his displaced blame. When she pointed out that I hadn't put the bottle to his lips, Ben became enraged and stormed out of the office, leaving me behind. That's when I promptly burst into tears and asked for an antidepressant prescription.

By year four, I no longer recognized myself. Ben's alcohol-fueled degradations had changed me into something akin to a scared mouse. Though I still loved him, I was finally beginning to acknowledge that he was not going to change. It was time to consider divorce.

This thought was distasteful, as I had said vows before God and families and I took them seriously. But what was even more abhorrent were the thoughts of suicide that were starting to overshadow my other options. These thoughts not only went against my moral code; they were terrifying.

Please God, let this agony just go away, I prayed as I sat on the carpeted steps leading to our bedroom, my eyes clamped shut and my hands cradling my downturned face. I was at the end of my tether by that time, and the words were fueled more by desperation than faith. Little did I know that my prayers had been heard and would soon be answered.

One night, after drinking ourselves pretty at a golf tournament, Ben and I joined a few teams at a local watering hole. The usual suspects were there, including the gregarious Amy and her tolerant fiancé. Amy was easy to like, a giggle box with a big personality who loved her booze and talking smack. But that night, she and Ben would take the fun too far and cross an invisible line.

While animatedly talking by the blackjack table, Amy reached over and grabbed my husband's bait and tackle. She gave it a good shake and her hand remained for several seconds as she squealed something or another to him with an open-mouthed laugh.

Though she was certainly hard to ignore, it wasn't Amy I was watching. I was looking at my husband's face, at the bloodshot, unfocused eyes searching the room for mine. When they found me, his expression became belligerent and challenging; his mouth curved into a smirk as he awaited my reaction.

God, I *hated* who Ben became when he drank. The reserved and respectful man I loved disappeared, leaving a rude, crass, and emotionally abusive stranger in his place.

As I took in his antagonistic gaze and cruel, crooked smile, I found my breaking point. Becoming unnaturally calm, a gift I've always had when under extreme duress, my smile faded, and I theatrically blinked my eyes as if to clear the hurtful image. I then let them fall to the ground as I reached for my belongings.

It was then that I saw others noticing. Their eyes moved from Amy and Ben to me and then back to them. Everything seemed to move in slow motion; the noisy and packed bar suddenly seemed deathly quiet.

I wanted to scream like a banshee. I wanted to pummel Ben for humiliating me in public. Even more so, I wanted to rail at him for committing adultery and breaking our sacred marriage bonds. Instead, fearing for my sanity and not wanting to see any pitiful looks, I returned my gaze to the floor.

I had to walk past them to get to the door and as I did, Ben extended his arm as if to stop me. This lame gesture was the equivalent of trying to stop a raging bull with a flyswatter and I easily pushed past him. Quickening my pace, I left the bar and ran to the car. As it purred to life, my headlights illuminated a familiar form. While Ben was walking towards me, *RUN HIM DOWN* roared through my mind. Obeying, my lips parted in a snarl as I tightened my grip on the steering wheel. At that moment, I was feral, and his existence was a risk to my survival.

Through squinted eyes, I glared at him and pressed the accelerator. *If I hit him then so be it,* I thought. *The stupid ADULTEROUS fucker!* What stopped me and maybe saved his life, was the sensation of prickling tears. As they filled my burning eyes, humanity returned, and I took my foot off the pedal.

Ben, in a vain attempt to stop the slowing car, tried grabbing the sideview mirror. As his hands slipped, I scoffed and thought, *As if.* I pressed the gas pedal, slowly this time, and glanced in the rearview mirror where I saw him standing with his arms half-raised as if to say, "What the hell?!"

Like you don't know, buddy.

By the time I pulled out of the parking lot, my driver's side window was open and I was gulping mouthfuls of air.

"Please God," I whimpered. "Please. Just get me home safely before I break wide open."

Luckily, home was only minutes away. Pulling into the garage, I grabbed the spare key from its hiding place and stumbled inside. Tears and giant sobs were threatening to take over as I locked the door and double-checked the front one. Confident that Ben was unable to enter, I crawled up the same stairs where I had, just days earlier, wondered what to do about my marriage.

A few whimpers escaped my throat as I entered our bedroom and locked the door, a precaution in case Ben did gain entry. Racing to the walk-in closet, I shoved my shirts and sweaters apart, slid into the corner and pulled my knees into my chest, making myself as small as possible. It was only then, while in this artificial cocoon of safety, that I let loose a subhuman howl of anguish.

The sound was filled with shattered dreams and smashed hopes, as well as fear and grief. Accompanying it, finally, were unrestrained, wailing cries, with snot flowing unchecked from my nose just as freely as the tears ran from my eyes. Sobs soon turned to hyperventilation, and, lightheaded and curled in a ball, I began mewling, "I want my mom. I want my mom!" I was thirty-six years old.

That was just the first wave. The next one had me hitting the floor with my fists, as I let loose a torrent of expletives that would have made the proverbial sailor blush. Throwing my head back, a scream that sounded as if it came from somewhere south of Hell ripped from my throat. That was the pinnacle of my storm, and when my head righted, a new me had been birthed. Drawing in cleansing, calming breaths, I focused on the anger that was pushing me into action.

Just then, the doorbell rang, followed by a pounding on the front door.

"Melissa!" I heard my husband call out. "Let me in! I can't find the key."

That's because I took it, you fucker. You fucking fucker.

"Melissa! Open up! I want to talk! What you saw wasn't . . ."

He droned on in the chilly night while I remained curled up in the back of our closet. My earlier hatred resurfaced, and in that moment I actually wished him dead. Maybe he'd freeze to death, I thought, and then my pain would be over. Similar thoughts were forming when the persistent doorbell brought me back to the problem at hand. Quickly switching my loathing to the chimes, I thought, *My fucking life has just exploded and the Goddamn doorbell won't shut the hell up!* In the end, though, that noise brought me out of my hidey-hole.

By that time, the venom seemed to have drained out of me. Now, as I parted my sanctuary and crawled out, I wiped away the last remaining tears, smoothed the wrinkles from my rumpled jeans and thought that not only was I exhausted, I felt as though I had aged ten years.

Slowly, I retraced my steps and opened the front door. I didn't look at Ben as he walked inside, and when he said he wanted to talk all I could do was mumble a flat, "Not now. I can't talk about this now. I need time."

Ignoring me, he tried to explain what I had witnessed. Knowing I would have done the same thing were I in his shoes, I merely put up my hand, palm out, and softly said, "Stop. Just stop. I can't. I just can't. I have nothing to give right now. Please leave me alone."

Leaving him in the foyer, I sluggishly began ascending the stairway once again. He grabbed my arm, intending only to turn me around, but his touch caused me to lose what little composure I had remaining. And, like a rabid dog, I attacked.

"LEAVE ME THE FUCK ALONE!" I screamed; my face contorted with rage. "ARE YOU A FUCKING IDIOT?! I CAN*NOT* DO THIS RIGHT NOW! LEAVE. ME. ALONE!"

His face was full of pain, but I was past the point of caring. Yanking my arm free, I raced for the safety of our bedroom. Crying, I clicked the flimsy lock, knowing it wouldn't keep him out if he really wanted in, but I hoped the noise would signify that he should not follow and that this was the beginning of the end.

Climbing into bed, I stared at the ceiling as tears continued seeping from my eyes. Turning on my side, I looked at Ben's empty pillow and caressed the space where his head and body should have been. Then, laying on my tummy, I screamed into my pillow while battering the mattress with my fists and feet. This pattern continued until the morning's light when, with swollen, blood-shot eyes, I looked out the window and wondered what the day would bring.

As he readied for work, Ben did not try to make contact. Shortly after he left, I roused myself and began slowly walking from room to room. I knew I would not be here much longer, and I wanted to take one last look at the house we called home. While doing so, the phone rang, and I absently glanced at the caller ID. What I saw caused me to freeze; it was none other than Amy, the groin-grabber from the night before. I stared at the device like it had morphed into a snake and thought, *You've* got *to be kidding me.*

But, on the fourth ring, right before it would have gone to the answering machine, I answered.

"Melissa!" she gushed. "I am so sorry about last night! *Please* do not divorce Ben because of what I did. PLEASE! It was harmless, and it was all me. I crossed the line and I am so sorry. Are you gonna divorce him?"

"I don't know what I'm gonna do," I said, my voice void of emotion. "And, yes you did cross the line and I'm not sure I'm ready to forgive you for that yet. And as far as divorce goes, that's for me and my husband to figure out."

After enduring another apology from Amy, I ended the call feeling no better than I had a moment earlier. Amy wasn't the problem; Ben was. Letting out a sigh, I knew he would apologize and swear to never do it again. I also knew that I would believe him because I desperately wanted it to be true.

These thoughts were swirling through my mind as I read through my journals. As if the night before wasn't enough, I was seeking additional reassurances that ending our marriage was the right thing to do. Forever thankful that I chose to document these experiences, I easily found all that I needed, and then some.

With certainty, I knew nothing was going to change because my husband didn't believe *he* was the one with the alcohol problem. According to him, I was the one with the problem, and on that, he was partially right.

That night Ben came home sober, but I knew it wouldn't last. *Same cycle, different day*, I thought as I retreated to the bedroom without saying a word. As my pain turned into contempt, I fell back on the tried and true methods my family always used to show their displeasure: being passive-aggressive and utilizing the silent treatment. I didn't know any other way.

A day passed and then two: he was still sober, and I was still quiet. I could see the misery my silence was causing him, for he had once again turned back into the man I loved. Embarrassed by his actions and feeling terrible that he had caused me so much suffering, he asked if we could talk and clear the air, but I was still too broken and raw to answer. It would have been kind of me to tell him this, but I didn't have anything to give.

Finally, on day three I was ready, and with a clear mind, I made peace with my decision and was committed to the next step. But, as it turned out, Ben was past begging me to discuss it and had decided to give me a taste of my own medicine.

Arriving home and without so much as a hello, he passed by me, went downstairs and started watching television. Knowing the gravity of the situation and that everything was about to change, I slowly followed and stood in front of him.

After making eye contact, I could tell he was now angry with me and again, I couldn't blame him. As his eyes dismissed me and returned to the TV, I gathered my courage. Clasping my shaking and clammy hands, I took a deep breath and said the four words that would end our marriage.

His eyes snapped back to mine and he laughed, though it sounded more like a bark. Did he think I was joking? I felt my own anger rekindling.

"Don't you threaten me with that," he snarled as he stabbed the air with his finger.

To appear bigger than I felt, I put my hands on my hips and squared my shoulders.

"Do you honestly think I would joke about this?!" I spat. "I. Want. A. Divorce."

Without waiting for his reaction, I ran up the stairs, slammed the bedroom door and threw myself on the bed. Knowing I had fought the good fight but had lost my husband – and marriage - to a seductress called Alcohol, I cried myself to sleep.

CHAPTER 2

Despite my show of bravado, I had abandonment and betrayal issues that made it extremely difficult for me to leave our marriage. Yet within two months of that fateful conversation, I signed a year lease and moved into an apartment. Days later, I was informed my job was being eliminated. I was lucky, HR told me; if this had happened just one month later, I would have received only six months of severance pay instead of thirteen.

Feeling anything but lucky, I panicked as another piece of stability, this time a twenty-one-year career, was coming to an end. At the same time, I knew this was a good thing, because although I liked my job, I didn't love it and Ben still worked there, a complication that neither of us needed. A change was necessary, I just hadn't expected it to be so sudden or without my involvement.

As divorces go, it was quick and easy, but not painless. How could it be, when you're ripping apart something you had intended to cultivate for a lifetime? We didn't fight or haggle over our assets, as some couples do. I told Ben I didn't want any spousal support and he said that was good because he wasn't going to give me any. On a frigid day in late January, less than four months after my declaration, our divorce was final.

After leaving the courthouse, I thought about stopping at a liquor store but went to my apartment instead. How was I supposed to feel? Was I celebrating or commiserating? Was I happy or sad? I was happy to be away from the abuse, but I achingly missed the kindness and love of my sober husband. I was sad to have a failed marriage, but happy that I didn't have any regrets; I knew I had done everything I could to try to save it. At the end of the day, still conflicted, I decided it was okay to feel both happy and sad and, in that, I found peace.

That peace was short-lived, however. Years of tiptoeing around emotional landmines had resulted in a severe case of PTSD, and in the coming weeks and months I found myself worrying about when the next life-changing event would happen. One day, unable to take the stress any longer, I broke into laughter that bordered on mania.

"What's next God?! Huh? Obviously, You wanted me to make some changes and You sure know how to get a girl's attention. So, what's next? Leprosy? Blindness? What?!"

I didn't have to wait long for the answer.

CHAPTER 3

"Well, Melissa, you have stage four cervical precancer."

I stared at my doctor like she had monkeys flying out of her butt. "I have what? Caa-caa-cancer?"

"Precancer," she corrected. "You are one stage away from it becoming cancerous. We'll need to perform a LEEP."

"Um, if you do that, will I still be able to have kids?"

Meeting my eyes, she replied, "No. Probably not. Your cervix has somewhat atrophied and it may not be able to form an effective seal."

Swallowing hard, my heartbeat quickened, and my eyes fell to the floor. Was this the fate of a woman who had never done illegal drugs because she was afraid of how they would affect her children? With a sense of injustice, my fear was replaced by indignance.

No way in hell am I accepting that answer. I'm not letting this ruin my chances of having a baby.

I swallowed again, raised my eyes and without any of the internal fire I was feeling, politely answered, "Okay. Um. Thank you."

I don't remember leaving the doctor's office; nor do I remember if we scheduled the procedure. What I *do* remember is racing to my apartment because I was the only one in the universe without a cell phone and I needed to talk this through with Rya. Without stopping to wash my hands (a true emergency!), I dialed her number.

"OH MY GAAAAAWD!" I blurted out as soon as she answered, "I HAVE CERVICAL PRECANCER! WHAT AM I GONNA DO?!"

Without waiting for her reply, I barreled on, "My doctor said that if I have this procedure, I won't be able to have kids. Oh my God. I *want* kids! At least I want the option. What do I do?!"

"Well, I don't know," Rya replied in her customary hushed tone. "Call Susie. She does Reiki. Maybe that will help."

I had no idea how those seemingly simple words would dramatically change my life, nor did I know that out of something "bad," something good would come, but I would understand this truth soon enough.

CHAPTER 4

I had met Rya several months prior to the end of my marriage. She was a personal trainer and one of the gym's cycling instructors. She had a soft voice that commanded your attention and I often marveled at how she could whisper directives and everyone would listen.

After the death of my marriage, I needed to feel strong again, both physically and emotionally. Thinking Rya could help me with the physical part, I contacted her and scheduled a series of personal training sessions. Little did I know that she would satisfy both my needs and an unbreakable bond of friendship would be forged.

Rya was young, almost twelve years younger than me, but she carried herself with poise, confidence and professionalism. We soon discovered we had a lot in common and our friendship quickly outgrew the confines of the gym. We started meeting for coffee, and before long I was being regularly invited to have supper with her, her husband and their young daughter. We watched movies, drank wine, laughed, and ate wonderful vegetarian food. During the week I continued to receive personal training, but on the weekends we would go for walks or practice yoga in her small living room and giggle whenever the videotape narrator incorrectly said "pubics" bones.

It was during one of these treasured walks that she taught me the 80/20 rule: eat healthy eighty percent of the time and do what you want with the rest. The first time I saw this health-conscious, well-mannered woman shoveling ice cream directly from the gallon container into her mouth, I did a double-take. Rya, her cheeks as full as a gathering gopher, had caught my surprised look and gave me an impish grin.

As our trust grew, we freely shared our secrets and beliefs; no topics were taboo. Rya told me how she wanted to live her life doing what felt right to her, not what family or society expected of her. If she was invited somewhere, she didn't just accept and then pray for a natural disaster, like I did. Instead, she would think about it and if it still didn't feel right, she would decline.

Her way of thinking and doing things had a profound effect on me. Having been raised to do things out of obligation, I went to church, worked a traditional job, put up with abusers and smiled when I felt like crying. Rya opened my eyes to another way of living, a way in which everyone could feel empowered.

Because of this, I started examining why I did certain things. For instance, did I send out Christmas cards because I wanted to or because I felt I had to? Did I suffer through an event with people I didn't like because it was expected? Did I continue to buy birthday cards for an abrasive family member because "that's what you do"? The answers to these and other questions both surprised and motivated me to make some changes.

One of my first was to reduce Christmas giving. As my extended family grew, gifts were purchased for people I barely knew, leaving me filled with stress instead of joy. No longer wanting to feel as if I was simply filling a quota, and daring to go against the grain, I told my family I wasn't buying Christmas presents anymore. Not surprisingly, I was met with confusion, but I held my ground and started a new tradition that was right for me.

Then, feeling proud of myself for having taken that courageous first step, I noticed that each subsequent act wasn't as scary and that I was becoming happier.

Rya subtly continued sharing her wisdom during the blissful, alcohol and laughter-fueled weekends we spent at her parents' lake cabin.

Sometimes, after either too many apricot brandy slushes or too much time in the sun, we woke with hangovers, but that didn't detour us from practicing yoga in the lake or skinny dipping in the moonlight.

During our time together, I surreptitiously watched how she parented and again noticed how vastly different it was from the way I was raised. She shared with me that she often ignored her young daughter's occasional meltdowns because forcing her child to go to her room would only add fuel to the fire; sometimes it was best to let her cry it out. When I questioned her about it, she explained that there were two or three reasons her daughter acted this way and none of them had anything to do with disrespect. Rather they were the result of low blood sugar, having too much processed sugar, or simply because she was tired. When she did need to reprimand, Rya used the same subdued but firm voice she used during spin class, but this time it was filled with love.

This, too, was in sharp contrast with my upbringing, and it showed me yet again that another way was possible. That way represented the person I was becoming, rather than the one I was leaving behind.

Rya, a lioness in a five-foot-two body with eyes so dark they appear black, was one of the catalysts for my transformation; the other was Susie, the woman Rya suggested I call.

CHAPTER 5

I need to share how in my younger years I was hungry for all things "psychic." I sought out readings, including palm and tarot card spreads, and was an occasional phone client of Dionne Warwick's Psychic Friends Network. In Fargo, my favorite psychic was Esmeralda, a transplant with a decidedly un-Scandinavian accent.

I'd met Esmeralda through a friend and liked her immediately. Having put psychics on a pedestal, I found she had an endearing ditziness that made her human and approachable. During our frequent sessions she was often a bit preoccupied and scattered, which only added to her genuineness and mystique. Sometimes she would appear freshly showered, her thick, long dark brown hair still wet and her face devoid of makeup. Other times she would be roused from sleep by the doorbell as she had, once again, forgotten to set her alarm. Still other times she would double book clients, which meant she would have to pick which one of us she saw. Then, once in session, she would conspiratorially giggle that I was her favorite and she was wearing a long skirt to hide her unshaven legs.

Esmeralda's psychic abilities, however, were no laughing matter, and I was immediately envious of her gifts. Peering at the tarot card spread, she knew my unspoken questions and wasted no time in giving me the answers.

"You are going to divorce your husband and he will never remarry. You are one in a million and he will never find anyone else like you. He will seek, but he will not find."

Then, tapping a card and with a sympathetic voice, she continued, "Ahhh. I see that you still love him."

My heart caught and my eyes filled with tears. "I don't think I do."

Briefly looking at me, she dismissed my words with a flick of her wrist. "Yes, this is true. You do still love him. You will always love him, but you will divorce."

Hearing those words, spoken so matter-of-factly, wrecked my fragile emotional state and, filled with an odd combination of despair and hope, I started crying. From behind the card table, Esmeralda rose and consoled me with a hug.

"It will be okay," she said simply.

"Will there be anyone else for me, or am I destined to be alone?" I asked through tears and sniffles.

"Yes, there will be another," she said as she stroked the back of my head. "He is not ready for you yet so maybe he is still married. And he will be, how you say . . . spicy? Yes. He will be very spicy. He has had a lot of women."

And then, with an astonished face, she repeated, "A *lot* of women."

Because she had accurately predicted the death of my marriage, among other things, I became dependent upon Esmeralda's psychic information. Desperately seeking reassurances and terrified that I would somehow mess up her prophecy and miss my chance at love, I scheduled weekly sessions during which she would take my money and assure me that nothing had changed.

I'd leave feeling buoyant and confident but within days, or sometimes hours, I'd feel as if I was drowning and she was the life preserver.

During one of these neurotic episodes, she offhandedly suggested that I purchase a magic crystal that she had extensively researched. The gemstone, according to her, resonated with me and was so powerful it could simultaneously clear my negative energy, past life karma, *and* help me find my One. Her sales pitch was a thing of understated beauty. It was as if she earnestly wanted all my desires to come true, not just fatten her pocketbook.

I swallowed all of it, partly because I didn't want to disappoint her and partly because I desperately wanted to believe what she was telling (selling?) me. I foolishly trusted she had my best interests at heart. Secretly though, I was afraid of the bad mojo I thought she could impose if I didn't do as she asked.

And she asked a lot. I sewed curtains for her apartment windows and made centerpieces for her sister's wedding because she *insisted!* There was no denying her, even when I tried. I didn't even know how to sew or to make centerpieces, for pity's sake, and yet I did it!

Looking back, I gave away too much of my power and I most definitely gave her *way* too much power.

So now I tell you, still somewhat red-faced more than eighteen years later, that I spent *one thousand dollars* on what would become an expensive paperweight. And even though stones do contain healing properties, my mind was vastly superior; I believed it had the power to heal and so it did.

Today, from a place on a closeted shelf, it serves as a reminder of what I will never do to those who seek my services. When I look at it, I remember how gullible people can be when they are grasping for their own life preserver.

About three months after I purchased the all-powerful crystal, Esmeralda suggested I buy, for another thousand dollars, two white tapered candles that she had infused with healing energy. She said they would get rid of the crud I had around me. *Crud?* When I meekly questioned her as to why I would need the candles when I had the mac daddy of stones, she, without missing a beat, said they would serve as "a good complement" to that.

Humm. I was divorced, unemployed, had bills to pay, and needed to make my savings last. I also had a small financial nest egg that was not to be touched, except in cases of emergency. She psychically knew about this and suggested I tap into it. This time, however, like a fish who had survived another season, I didn't bite. *A thousand dollars for two candles that were going to burn and disappear?* (Head scratch) *No. Just no. I'm not gonna do it.*

When I told her just that, she insisted I *needed* them. During previous sessions, she had instructed me to buy a rainbow-colored blanket and her homemade multi-colored bath salts. I was comfortable with these requests, as well as paying for our sessions, because they were all modestly priced. But another thousand dollars? That was where I drew the line. *Sorry, Esmeralda.*

When she sensed she no longer had a live one on the hook, she, like any good salesperson, sweetened the deal. Her offer to negate any future session fees did give me pause, but I continued to stand my ground. Then another attempt was made, and the same response was given.

After that, our appointments became less and less frequent, and although I still valued and relied on her psychic abilities, my trust in her had begun to fade. In addition to that, the quirks I had once found endearing were now an irritant. Others may have felt the same way because within four months of refusing to buy the candles, I arrived for an appointment and discovered that she, as well as her furnishings and flashing neon PSYCHIC sign, were gone.

Like the gypsy she was, she had simply vanished into the night.

CHAPTER 6

Susie is a true force of nature. Standing well over six feet, she has never been one to self-consciously slump her shoulders or detract from her height; in fact, she often wears high heels. With or without them, people will remark, "Woah! You're tall!" to which she proudly says, "Yeah! I am!"

Regardless of her physical stature, Susie has an undeniable presence. Her demeanor is soothing, her voice is calming and because of this, I long ago gave her the nickname "Aloe Vera."

It was Susie who, while I was a client, continuously told me I was so *freaking* intuitive." She saw something in me that I was blind to, encouraged me to reconnect with my gifts and to begin journaling again. Susie, who calls herself an *intuitive,* was also the exact opposite of Esmeralda and other psychics I had gone to.

A case in point was during one of our sessions, when Susie relayed that my Other was near. As time passed and he hadn't appeared, my patience disintegrated, and I began to fear that I had missed the opportunity. Seeking reassurances, and apparently a sucker for punishment, I went to another psychic.

Our interaction was brief because she soon revealed herself to be a truly vile and opportunistic person who tried to capitalize on my insecurities and loneliness. Finding out I was there for a "love/commitment" reading, she raised the price, set a loudly ticking – and very distracting - egg timer and then began eating a fast food hamburger.

With her mouth full, she said my soulmate would never be in my orbit if I didn't clear my karma.

Luckily, though, she had the elixir. Showing me an array of small bottles that contained colorful bath salts, she selected one and said, "Five-hundred dollars if you buy right now. One-thousand if you wait until the end of session."

"I don't have that kind of money," I stammered.

"Then you will never find your soulmate."

Disgusted with her and disappointed in myself, I left her office before my time was finished. *Thank God I didn't fall for that line of crap.* My thoughts then turned to those who would, and I felt a pang of sadness. The woman was indeed an apex predator.

But I did fall for some of what she was slinging. A seed of doubt was planted and even though nothing about our meeting felt right, I couldn't help but wonder, *What if?* Once home, and without hesitation, I dialed Susie's number and began praying, *Please be home, Susie. Please. Please pick up. Pick uuuhhhhhhp!*

Susie answered and upon hearing the distress in my voice, gave me her full attention.

"Honey, oh, sweetie. No. No. You get to choose who you believe, *what* you believe. You get to make your own truth and I'm telling you, he *is* coming for you. You don't need expensive products, you just need to trust. Honey. No. You're beautiful and strong and have come so far. Focus on that, okay?"

When we ended the call, I thought about how Susie would never sell me a thousand-dollar placebo or cause me to fear. She chose to use her gifts differently, with empowerment and translucence. And even though my reading others' energy was still on the horizon, I clearly felt her love and integrity shine through during each of our interactions.

From that day forward, wanting to set myself apart from those who had threaded fear into the fabric of my life, I would refer to myself as an intuitive, just like my mentor.

CHAPTER 7

During yet another session, Susie stopped translating the telepathic words in mid-sentence and lowered her head into her hands. When she raised it, she announced that our guardian angels ("The Guys" as she - and I - affectionately call them) were becoming exhausted. It seems that with all my questions and "show mes" I had succeeded in testing their normally inexhaustible patience.

Looking at me from beneath her knitted eyebrows, Susie appeared amazed by their frustration, while I felt only embarrassment. *Uh huh, yes, leave it to me to confound the angels.* Formerly an internal auditor, I was highly analytical and had yet to learn about trusting in things that weren't tangible.

I scrunched my shoulders and protested. "But I just wanna know the answers to *everything!*"

"All in good time," Susie said with a smile. "Look at it like this: you are a toddler and need to learn at that rate. You can't expect to understand collegiate answers until you are at that level. If the Guys downloaded all the answers to the questions you've been asking, your brain would explode. You - meaning 'we' - just can't handle too much of that kind of knowledge. Trust that it will all come to you when you are ready and not a moment before."

Susie went on to say that I needed to ask for help, not only from my fellow humans but from my astral team as well. This was a new concept for me because I had spent a lifetime thinking others should just know what I needed. Unfortunately, it doesn't work that way on earth or in heaven. You have to *ask.*

When Rya suggested I call Susie about my medical diagnosis, I didn't think twice. Susie and I had developed a professional friendship by this time and it only made sense to ask for her help. When she answered, I rapidly and in a disturbingly high-pitched voice, explained what the doctor had told me.

"Susie? Do you think you can help me?"

"I've seen some miracles through Reiki, Missy Pooh," she replied confidently. "Let's get you set up for a Group Healing."

When that night came, I was nervous. I didn't know what to expect (which screams *Danger!* to us controlaholics) as I had never experienced Reiki before and it hadn't dawned on me to research it.

Now I know that Reiki is a twenty-five-hundred-year-old Japanese technique for reducing stress and promoting healing. In a nutshell, Reiki is energy work and the energy goes where it is most needed. It's not up to the practitioner to control the flow of energy - that's done by a Higher Power (God, Source, or Universe – whatever you feel comfortable with), who can see your entire life's blueprint. The practitioner is merely a conduit; the heavy lifting is done by The Man/Woman/Being Upstairs in agreement with the soul of the person receiving Reiki. Reiki can never harm and all who receive it reap some benefit, whether it can be seen or not.

I entered Susie's large office cautiously and quietly. Her rented space was decorated with personality: original artwork, an antique desk, mismatched chairs, colored vases and lots of books. The eclectic effect was both inviting and soothing.

There were about ten Reiki practitioners milling around and chatting. I felt overwhelmed and humbled that they would give their time to help me, someone they'd never met. I was struggling with self-worth issues, so I didn't believe I was deserving of their help. *These must be a special breed of people,* I thought. I would later understand that once you've learned Reiki, you become hardwired to share it.

One of the rooms contained a massage table, and when Susie asked me to lie on it I didn't hesitate. Somebody handed me a quilt Susie's grandmother had made in the 1930s. With soft pink flowers and an off-white background, it was well-aged. Susie referred to it as her "healing quilt" and once underneath it, my earlier jitters felt more manageable.

Standing next to me, the practitioners placed their hands lightly upon my body and I was shocked to feel heat emanating from them. *What the hell?* My eyes, already wide and alert, searched their faces for any sign that this was disturbing to them. Finding none, and though I was still somewhat uncomfortable being administered to, I began to relax under the soothing heat and the sound of their comfortable chatter. After a few minutes, some of them changed positions and stood elsewhere by my body.

A short twenty minutes later the Group Healing concluded. Sitting up, I turned my arms slowly and examined them to see if they were still flesh. Was I different? I didn't feel any different and yet I knew something *powerful* had happened. Reiki, in its infinite wisdom, was working on my damaged emotional self as well as helping to heal my outdated thoughts, insecurities and negative self-beliefs. It was also working towards helping me understand I was healthy, happy and whole even though I currently felt the opposite.

As I hopped off the massage table, I continued to marvel at how selfless these energy workers were. Feeling indebted and aware that a bond had been forged, I thanked each one of them with words and hugs. As I was leaving, I knew I needed one more Group Healing. Not exactly sure why I was feeling that way but unwilling to go against it, I asked Susie if we could plan one more get together in a month's time. Without hesitation, she agreed.

Four weeks later, I found myself back in Susie's office. Right from the start, things were different. The assembled practitioners were different. The energy of the Healing was different. Most importantly, I was different. The only things that felt the same were the massage table and the weathered quilt.

Now knowing what to expect, I was much more relaxed and even closed my eyes and allowed myself to rest. These practitioners were subdued and in the quiet, I drifted into a light sleep. At one point, I thought I was levitating and was about to touch the ceiling with my nose. This sensation was so real that I would have bet dollars to donuts on it, but when my eyes snapped open and took in my surroundings, I saw that my body was on the table.

Throughout the session I felt warmth everywhere, not just where the practitioner's hands were, and the feeling of floating weightlessly remained. I was also moved to tears and didn't know why. Powerless to stop them, they flowed freely – a big no-no for someone who had learned through example that crying makes you appear weak and should only be done in private.

When the Healing was finished, I felt both drained and invigorated, heavy and light, solid and transparent. I also felt as if I had been restored. And with that, a deep sense of peace came over me, as did a knowing that my precancerous condition was gone.

This was confirmed a month later after a follow-up exam. My doctor, a woman of science, was both amazed and puzzled because, as she put it, this "just doesn't happen." Her words caused me to smile and filled me with a sense of wonder. Over a three-month span, I had diligently worked on healing emotional wounds and changing how I viewed myself. Her statement not only validated my intuition and hard work but also supported the healing power of Reiki.

Out of this health scare, and the events that followed, I would find what I had been seeking for so long: my true calling.

CHAPTER 8

Sensing there was more to Reiki than met the eye, and with the miracle of my precancerous healing still fresh, I started thinking that maybe God *did* have a plan for me, and maybe that plan was to experience how powerful Reiki was so I would start doing energy work professionally.

As I contemplated this – and inched closer to a decision not to return to Corporate America - I thought, *If I can take away someone's pain, even for five minutes, I will consider myself a huge success.* My mind then traveled to my dad; however, it would be years later until I understood why.

These thoughts led me to enroll in an introductory Reiki class taught by Susie and then, enjoying both the education and the teacher, I decided to continue. While learning about (and practicing) Reiki, I worked a few fun part-time jobs in order to network and bring in a little money. I was still unsure as to where my earlier revelation would lead or what my "real job" would be, so I chose instead to focus on feeling stronger and letting go of some internal afflictions that seemed to follow me.

As a child whose lineage contains both alcoholism and addiction, I knew how to manipulate and control. Neither of those attributes had served me well and I didn't want them to be a part of my life as I moved forward. With the help of Reiki, I began sifting through memories and beliefs, assimilating what resonated and discarding what didn't. Along with this spiritual purging came a physical one. Shortly after taking the second level of Reiki training, I had an emotional breakthrough that left me crying so hard I vomited.

While I was vested in my healing, I had discovered it was a lonely place. I had been divorced for over three years and had only dated one person. He was an oasis in my solitary world and treated me like a princess. We both knew it wouldn't last, though. I wanted kids and he had already raised his. I wasn't much of a drinker, and he was. He liked the nightlife and I was more of a homebody. When we parted ways, I found myself with a heartache and a heightened sense of relationship standards and I knew I would always be thankful to – and for - him.

Once again, Rya and her small family did a great job of keeping me entertained, but, inevitably, I would leave them and face my empty apartment. My recently ended relationship aside, I felt like I had been by myself for too long. In fact, it felt like a continuation of the great loneliness I had experienced within the confines of my marriage. Holding tight to what Susie and Esmeralda had told me, I *knew* someone was coming for me, but *where was he already?*

As time moved on, my spiritual growth and healing continued. I had learned how to meditate, which was quite the feat for this spinning mind, and I was tentatively trying to communicate with guardian angels. Reading books by Sylvia Brown, James Van Praagh and Echo Bodine kept my mind engaged while my body was delving deeper into yoga. I continued examining emotions and memories, weeding out what no longer had value and keeping what did. And finally, I was playing with Doreen Virtue's, "Healing with the Fairies" and "Healing with the Angels" tarot cards where every spread affirmed I was changing, healing and that romance was coming for me.

Journaling exactly what I wanted in a soulmate, I described his temperament; the sort of father he would be to our children; how he would treat me and others. At least once a week, and sometimes once a day, I would look at these words and then close my eyes, holding them in my thoughts. Then I would meditate, trying to draw his ethereal image into reality. Sometimes, during those still moments, I was even able to act as though he was already in my life.

No matter what was going on, I found time to incorporate a mantra into my day. I would be at the gym or taking a walk, repeating with each step, "I am healthy, happy and whole." At first, the words felt empty and mocking, but the more I repeated them, the more I believed. And still today, in times of struggle or confusion, these words cut through my mental cobwebs and remind me how far I've come. I am living proof that the mind believes what you tell it, positive or negative.

My days grew increasingly full of activities that were healing to the mind, body and soul. The nights, however, were another story. They seemed to last an eternity, especially during the winter months. Lighting candles, I would mindlessly zone out while watching television. Sometimes, when the quiet, the dark, and the solitude overwhelmed me (or when I was PMSing), I would raise my eyes to the ceiling, my mind screaming, *Where is he?!* WHERE IS HE?!

Then I started noticing I was hearing the same song, U2's "I Still Haven't Found What I'm Looking For," over and over. I would turn on the car radio and hear it playing, then after changing stations I would hear it again. And if it wasn't on the radio, it was on the television. This might not have been so odd if the song was new, but it wasn't; it had been released eight years earlier. Knowing this couldn't be a coincidence but not understanding the meaning, I started to get cranky. *Okay! I get it! I'm lonely and will be for a while because* I STILL HAVEN'T FOUND WHAT I'M LOOKING FOR! *Do you have to rub it in?*

I also started to notice the number three *everywhere.* I would wake up at 3:33. A voicemail time stamp would be 3:33. While traveling, highway mile marker 3, 33, or 333 would jump out at me. Rent a video? It had been rewound to the number 333. An infomercial phone number? 800-333-3333. My grocery or gas bill? $33.33 The mileage on my car? 33,333. After weeks of this, I was beyond exasperated when I purchased Doreen Virtue's book "Angel Numbers" in the hopes that it would shed some light. After looking up every variation of the number three, I was disappointed to realize the information didn't resonate.

Growing more perplexed by the day, I consulted with Susie who told me that our guardian angels *love* to communicate through numbers and songs. What she hadn't said was that you need to figure out the whys. As someone leery of trusting what I could not see, that part was endlessly frustrating.

"You can't see oxygen," Susie would say during her Reiki trainings, "and yet we all know it's there as we wouldn't be alive."

Jolly good. I'll just continue to be driven insane, I guess.

Then, one cold winter's night, I was curled up on the couch watching Grey's Anatomy (back when it was good) when my phone rang. *Who in the hell is calling me?* I thought, aggravated at the prospect of missing even one minute of the drama between Meredith and McDreamy.

The name didn't come up on caller ID, and that, along with crappy timing, would normally be enough justification for me not to answer. But for some reason, this time felt different. Torn, I glanced at the television, then back to the ringing phone, and on the third ring, I let out a sigh and answered.

The voice on the other end was male and unfamiliar. He was also, I would learn, the reason I had been seeing threes everywhere.

This caller's name was the literal embodiment of the number three. It means "Triad" or "Three in One," and is referred to in the bible and by millions of people, including myself, as "the Father, the Son and the Holy Ghost."

His name was *Trinity*.

CHAPTER 9

I had met Trinity (who was named not for anything religious but the 1971 Western "They Call Me Trinity") years earlier, when Ben and I were building our house. I had been hearing about him long before that, though, as he was a classmate and a good friend of my youngest niece, Jessica. Over the years she would tell me about their friendship and say that he was such a great guy. Then, after he was deployed to Saudi Arabia, she would ask me to pray. Following his return, she told me he was getting married; then later, that his marriage was a fiasco and he didn't deserve to be miserable.

Jessica lived in Fargo for a brief span of time, and one night she brought Trinity, also a Fargo resident, to the apartment where Ben and I lived. Trinity was youthful in appearance, with wide hazel eyes, a short, military-style haircut and an athletic build. I supposed some would think he was cute, but as he was six years my junior, I just thought of him as a nice "boy" who meant a lot to my niece.

I was wearing the most unflattering outfit in the world; a pair of high-waisted "mom" jeans, a turtleneck and a way-too-large windbreaker. Clearly, I was not dressed to impress and yet, that's just what I did.

With only my hands and face showing skin, I would have been shocked to learn that this "nice boy" saw through my figure-hiding clothes and was looking at me in a *sexual* way.

But he was.

Oh, I never would have known it from his face or demeanor; he was the epitome of politeness and respect. It would be several years later before he revealed to me how desirable he thought I was.

Apparently, I was *rockin'* those jeans.

But as I said, those steamy revelations were in the future. That night my mind was on the in-wall stereo system Ben and I wanted to install. Our builder had given us the names of someone they used and liked, one of which was Jason. He took great care of us but after the installation he handed us off to his business partner, Trinity. As in Jessica's Trinity. I kid you not.

When Trinity arrived for the service call, he was professional, above board and very knowledgeable. He gave us a tutorial on how to get the most out of our new purchase, made sure we were comfortable with it, and then left.

A few months later, I could not get the system's remote to work. After calling and explaining to Trinity the issue, he said, "Oh, bring it to the shop! I'll help you with it." Wasting no time, I got in my car (the same one I would later use to try to run down my husband) and drove to his place of employment. He was again cordial, competent and attentive, thus reinforcing my image of him.

Little did I know he was staring at my assets as I left the store.

Jessica continued to keep me informed of the drama going on in Trinity's life. The latest was he felt his wife went off birth control – and subsequently became pregnant - to try and keep him in their loveless marriage. Trinity, who was both excited and nervous about being a first-time father, filed for divorce a few months after his son was born. Though I felt a general empathy for another human in pain, I wasn't really all that interested in his saga. I barely knew the guy, and besides, I had my own marital showdown a-brewin'.

Never once did it occur to me that Jessica didn't share information about her other guy friends; nor did I find it odd that she shared *so much* about the personal life of Trinity. And when she mentioned he might be calling for some interior design advice, again, I thought nothing of it.

CHAPTER 10

"Hi Melissa!" he said that night on the phone. "This is Trinity." And with that, like the commercials for V8 juice, I had a forehead-slapping moment; *he* was the reason behind the threes. What I didn't know was *why,* but as the Guys had earlier stated, when I was ready for the answers, they would be revealed. Breathing an internal sigh of relief, I raised my eyes to the ceiling in a silent *thank you.*

Of course my voice didn't reflect any of that satisfaction when I said, "Why are you calling me during Grey's Anatomy? What is wrong with you?!"

"Is it Thursday?!" he replied without missing a beat. "I thought it was Wednesday. Shit. I like that show too. Should I call ya back?"

I giggled. "Nah. What's up?"

He had recently purchased a home and wanted me to come over and help him choose paint colors. Having a flair for interior design, I had briefly considered pursuing this as a career after banking, and I was happy to lend my knowledge.

Little did I know that while he had indeed bought a house, the request for help was just an excuse to call. During our three-hour conversation there wasn't a shortage of topics, and the communication flowed smoothly. Still viewing him as a "boy," I couldn't understand the repeated requests for me to come over immediately. I thought he was interesting, in a platonic way, and it wasn't until later that I realized he had been hoping to change that.

Before saying goodnight, we set up a day and time for the color consultation. He even offered to come and pick me up. When the day arrived, I readied my paint booklets and dressed professionally. After a tour of his post-divorce house, he opened a bottle of red wine, poured us each a glass and we discussed his ideas. And then, just like days earlier, the easy conversation turned to everyday events and was filled with laughter.

That all ended when, with a mischievous grin, he confessed, "When Jessica introduced us, and you bent down to pick up that carpet sample, it was almost more than I could take."

Taken aback by this unexpected revelation, I was trying to process his words when this "polite young man" suddenly turned into a human octopus. His hands were everywhere at the same time. As if that wasn't enough, he then used his tongue as if trying to perform a thorough examination of my tonsils.

What the bloody hell?

Standing there, unable to move and with eyes wide open like a deer caught in the headlights, I thought, *Gross! This is like kissing my kid brother. And God, he's a horrible kisser!* Still not in my right mind, I thought maybe I should kiss him back which was definitely *not* the way to go. *Lesson learned.* Not only was I repulsed by his passion, but I couldn't understand why he was so into this when I clearly was not. Then, when I realized he had lied - there never were any paint colors to pick out – my shock turned to anger, and my body mobilized.

With both hands I gave his solid chest a formidable push, then raised one hand to my lips and wiped my mouth.

"I am not ready for this type of intimacy!" I sputtered indignantly, then gave voice to what I had been thinking a few moments earlier. "Gross! It's like kissing my kid brother!"

Unruffled, he replied, "I've always found you so attractive and have thought about you a lot. I guess having you in my house, so near, well, I just wanted to kiss you."

Oh, you're smooth, little boy, I'll give you that, but I won't be a notch in your bedpost.

His clean-cut boyish image evaporated, and I knew he was lying again; *obviously* he wanted to do more than just kiss me.

With squinted eyes, I pushed past him. Grabbing my paint deck, I stomped down the stairs, retrieved my coat and with all the imperiousness of a queen, demanded to be taken home. Silence came from the upstairs level and as I waited, I wished I could see his dimple-cheeked face. Judging by his earlier bravado, I bet he was unaccustomed to rejection, and that it smarted like hell.

A moment later, Trinity appeared looking bewildered and we walked out to his vehicle. I saw him reaching out and, thinking he was ready for another round of "Octopus vs. Prey," I jumped backwards.

"I'm just opening the door," he said, but before he got any ideas, I huffed by him with all the haughtiness I could muster. Careful not to look at or touch him, I scooted into the passenger seat and slammed the door. As he slid behind the wheel, I secured my seatbelt and moved as far away from him as I could.

On the drive to my apartment he kept saying he didn't know what went wrong. He didn't know how he could have misread the signals.

Signals?

"In my defense," he added, "you kissed me back."

Don't remind me.

Despite his earlier ruse, I could tell this wasn't an act; Trinity was genuinely upset. The idea that he had wronged me really went against his grain. He was not built like that. He didn't have to take things from women who willingly gave them, and he wouldn't take things from women who didn't *want* to give them.

As he pled his case, I remained stoic and continued to try to be one with the door. When he pulled into the parking lot, I unbuckled my seatbelt and reached for the door handle. My other hand went for the door lock in case Doctor Tonsil Checker tried to schedule another exam. He didn't. In fact, he truly was a gentleman, but I could not see it. As I scurried out, I caught sight of his troubled face.

"I'm so sorry!" he said, but I had already slammed the door shut.

I marched into my apartment and when I locked the door, I noticed I was shaking from anger, and not just at Trinity.

"What in the HELL was *that*, Guys?!" I shouted to the solitary space. "What were you thinking, setting me up with that player . . . that octopus!? You've *got* to be joking! You sent me all those signs . . . all those number threes . . . and then I end up running from him? I don't, I don't understand!"

I was met with silence.

CHAPTER 11

My outrage lasted the entire night. Unable to sleep, I tossed and turned as I replayed the events in my mind, and then eventually got around to asking myself how I could have missed *his* signals. In hindsight, they were clear as day and I felt the fool for not having seen them sooner. The next morning when I turned my phone's ringer on, I saw I had missed a call and a voicemail from him. I felt a fresh wave of contempt bubbling to the surface.

Fuck off, Mr. Handsy McOctopus.

Needing some clarity, I emailed Susie. Her reply came within the hour.

"Missy Pooh! This isn't necessarily the disaster you think it is. It looks like Trinity is acting on the 'lover' energy between you two and you are acting on the 'goddess' energy."

In other words, I wanted to get to know his soul and he, apparently, wanted to get to know my vagina.

I continued reading. "I see a beautiful golden cord going between the both of you. Trinity really is a very sweet guy and if you can trust, and talk through it with him, it looks like everything will be fine. Also, you might try sending him the energy you want to receive."

Her words were soothing but they did little to calm me. In fact, they caused even more angst as it appeared that I needed to confront Trinity. Growing up, conflict often ended in angry words and physical punishment. Because of this, I never learned how to properly address miscommunications or disagreements. Now it looked as if I was going to be given an opportunity to change that.

But first, in an attempt to ignore what I needed to do, I went to the gym where I took out my frustration on a treadmill. When that didn't help, I tried yoga, and when *that* failed, I decided to give some serious thought to what Susie had written. Yet even as I considered talking this out with Trinity, I kept circling back to one thought: *Why bother?*

When I got home, I asked the Guys to show me three random threes by day's end if I was supposed to continue with Trinity. Within hours, I had my answer.

Since they had delivered, I listened to Trinity's message. Sounding contrite and truly apologetic, he asked if we could try this again and he promised to be on his best behavior. I returned his call, accepted his apology, and agreed to see him again providing there were some ground rules; no touching, no kissing and distance was to be maintained. Surprisingly, he agreed without hesitation. He must know when to fight and when to fold, I thought; either that or he was intrigued by the challenge I presented.

I drove to his house and, still cringing a bit from the last encounter, placed my key in my pants pocket for easy access. I also kept a wary eye on him as we moved from room to room with my color swatches. This time, there was no wine offered.

But even though he was sweet as pie and honoring the preset rules, I couldn't help but see him as a manipulative little boy who was used to getting what he wanted from the ladies. Admittedly, he was cute, and his dimpled smile was (cultivated to be) disarming. I bet many an unsuspecting lass had lost her virtue to his charms. I would be sure to give this one a wide berth.

Sharing stories of our childhood and telling safe secrets, we discovered we had lived in the same cities, albeit at different times. Our banter was fluid, our laughter was quick, and I couldn't shake the sense that I had always known him.

As the evening progressed without any appearances from Mr. Handsy or Dr. Tonsil Checker, I felt respected and heard. We agreed to see each other again but didn't schedule anything. As I left, unaccosted and with a smile on my face, I was glad that I had listened to both Susie and the Guys; Trinity was worthy of a second chance and while I wasn't ready to admit it, he was starting to intrigue me.

After three days of no contact, however, intrigue had turned into impatience. My late mother had ingrained in me that the boys should call me and that I didn't need to chase them. Her wisdom had worked well over the years, but this wasn't the '80s anymore and girls called guys all the time. Maybe I should too?

By day four, Mom's advice was quickly losing its luster and I decided to call Trinity. As my clammy hands picked up the phone, I partially dialed his number only to slam the receiver onto the base. Clasping my hands to my chest, I started jumping up and down like a Mexican jumping bean. Oh my GOD! What was I doing? This was almost *sinful.*

(Really, Melissa?!)

With a giggle and feeling a little like a rebellious teenager, I reached for the phone again. *What's the big deal? Just call him! It's not as if you're committing your life to him. Just call him, you big chicken!*

And so, I did. I dialed all the digits, let the phone ring and, wahhh wahhhh wahhhhh, I got his answering machine, something I was not prepared for. Panicking, I didn't know whether I should hang up or leave a message. *If I leave a message,* I thought, *what do I say?* Think. *Think.* THINK! Then his outgoing message ended, and I heard the beep. *Shit.* SHIT! Completely unprepared, I babbled something that was supposed to sound cool and casual but was anything but that. I then asked him to call and left my number, which, duh, he already had.

By the time I disconnected my mouth was dry and my heart was beating like a scared rabbit's. Good Lord, what was *wrong* with me? *Seriously*! How could violating some outmoded rule - and while in my early forties - cause me to feel so *naughty*? Then again, perhaps I wasn't spazzing out over that; maybe I was worried that I had over-played my hand. After all, he clearly enjoyed being the aggressor.

The next evening, after spending the day worrying myself into a snit, Trinity called. Upon hearing his voice, my apprehension dis-solved. He apologized for not returning my call sooner - he had injured his back and was unable to move.

"Oh! Do you need anything?" I asked in my best nursemaid voice. "I have this amazing Polar Ice rub that might help. And do you need aspirins? I can bring some over."

The reality was I wanted to see him again and those questions, while genuine, were as much of a ruse as his request for paint colors had been. As I said before, Trinity had gotten to me and I needed to know why. The only way to do that was to take a closer look.

Trinity accepted my offer and I wasted no time returning to the enigma's lair. The front door was unlocked, and when I entered his bedroom, I noticed he hadn't bothered to put on lounging pants. *Wear-ing only his boxers, well, that's a bit forward,* I thought. And then, *Humm. I'm really more of a boxer-brief kind of gal.*

Danger, *danger* Will Robinson! If I was assessing the clothing he was – or was not – wearing, I was no longer emotionally distant.

The wide berth I had given him was shrinking.

Our conversation flowed until we landed on our past romances. It was then, just as I had suspected, and as Esmeralda had foretold, Trin-ity confided that he had been very promiscuous.

He had a steady in high school and they would often meet in one of their vehicles for a quickie. When they broke up, he practiced only mild discernment and had his pick of the litter. Almost anywhere was fair game for sex: behind buildings, motel hallways, elevators, his work desk and, once, an army exam room.

And while I found all this scandalous, my jaw dropped when he added that more than once these scenarios happened daily and with different women. He joked that he'd done it all for me, in order to be the best that he could be.

This elicited giggles and some blushing from me, but as I would learn much later, the truth behind his behavior was no laughing matter. Trinity had been looking for a way to numb the emotional pain from his childhood, and sex was his drug of choice.

In turn, I shared with him that I had been referred to as "ice cold" by several potential conquests. Plain and simple, I just didn't put out. This, I would later learn, was my way of trying to protect myself from more abandonment.

After we had talked for what seemed like forever, I told him about a dream I'd recently had. I was frightened because he was working too much, which caused me to feel like I had in my marriage - lonely and abandoned. Interestingly, Trinity admitted that he had worked a lot but had really cut back. I left it at that but made a mental note to tell him how important it was that I feel, if we were to date, like a priority.

He then suggested we have a glass of wine. *Thought you'd never ask!* With filled glasses in hand and the open bottle on the nightstand, we sat on his queen-sized bed and talked and giggled. And even though the television was on, it was just background noise; we were all about each other.

That night, I discovered there was something vulnerable and authentic about him. Unable to figure it out, I caught myself staring at him out of the corner of my eye. I also noted that, as promised, he didn't raise a finger to touch me, even after I had gotten a little flirty.

"It must be so difficult for you to control yourself while you have the ultimate object of desire in your bed, yet you can't touch her."

He favored me with one of his disarming, heart-fluttering, impish smiles and said, "I could still take you, bad back and all. Even with both hands behind my back."

I downed the last of my wine and inwardly purred, *Ooooh, I bet you could, big boy.*

CHAPTER 12

While my fascination with Trinity began to grow, my savings account continued to shrink. Having been raised by parents who'd survived the thirties, I knew the value of money and the benefit of saving it. I had also learned, among other things, that I should scrape the last of the peanut butter out of the jar and wash and reuse bread bags. With this being an integral part of my upbringing, you can imagine watching my financial safety net dwindle day by day was causing me real anxiety. During an intuitive session, Susie had told me I would always have just enough money and that a job was right in front of me. Although I trusted her, I was terrified that I had somehow messed that up. I needed income, and soon!

That was the last thought I had before I fell asleep. That night, I dreamt that I was in fluffy white clouds which pulsated pastel colors. I was facing an arched doorway of some sort and while I didn't see anybody, I heard voices. Then, out of the corner of my eye, I saw someone standing near me and I shifted my gaze. She had shoulder-length white hair that was gently blowing away from her unseen face. When I moved my eyes back to the doorway, I was now standing in the spot she had occupied. I asked if I had missed the job opportunity, and she told me that I had, but not to fear because many doors were now opening, and the perfect opportunity would be coming soon. This felt right and I smiled as a sense of peace blanketed me.

CHAPTER 13

Something shifted in me after the flirty tete-a-tete in Trinity's bedroom. I found myself fantasizing about having sex with him. Say whaaat? First it feels like I'm kissing my brother and now I wanna bone him? *Domo arigato, Mr. Roboto.*

In mid-February, just a little over two weeks since this song and dance started, Trinity invited me over. As usual, we had an easy time of talking and discovering. Our interactions were completely chaste, which, despite my recent fantasies, was still just fine by me. After discussing decorating plans, we also decided that I was to spend the days painting and be gone by five, which was the time he returned with Ian, his four-year-old son.

In the past, this wouldn't have mattered because Trinity had been quick to introduce his "lady friends" to his son. But when Ian began asking questions about them, Trinity realized the interactions had impacted his son more than he thought, and because of this, he wasn't ready for us to meet. Instead of feeling hurt or insulted by this, it had the opposite effect: it meant that I was more than just a casual fling.

Whatever this relationship/non-relationship was, I found comfort in the fact that we were doing it differently by slowing things down. And even though we had not discussed it, we both knew that getting close quickly hadn't worked in the past. Intimacy would eventually happen, but for now we gave each other breathing room, dressed up for in-house dates and limited noisy bodily functions.

Happy with the direction we were going in and with paint plans finalized, we decided it was time to end another night. As I descended the stairs, coat in hand, Trinity asked if he could give me a goodnight hug, something that was now commonplace. Feeling safe, I agreed, and he gently enveloped me in a big, non-threatening, non-sexual hug. I thought he was, hands down, one of the best huggers I had ever known. Inside his arms, I felt protected and as if the outside world and its worries didn't exist. Contented to just be, I nuzzled my nose into the exposed skin of his neck and inhaled. And then something happened, something . . . *animalistic*. My nostrils flared, my pupils dilated, and all my senses were on heightened alert. As if it had been electrified, my body stiffened, and I breathed in his heady scent again. *Must be pheromones,* I thought, but why hadn't I smelled them before?

Then I did something unexpected; I lifted my head and kissed him fully on the lips.

I just wanted a peck; a quick, closed-lipped kiss, but the next thing I knew I was pushing him against a wall and grinding my lips into his like my life depended on it.

Somehow, I managed to regain control of my traitorous brain and pushed Trinity aside. With a confused smile and a shake of my head, I drew in a breath and tried to steady myself. Big mistake, because that was all the delay he needed. This time it was Trinity who pushed me against the wall and after more passionate kissing, I squirmed out of his grasp and made a break for the door. He was quicker and stopped me from leaving by crushing me to his chest and then pushing me backwards onto the steps.

Having fantasized about this very scenario, I realized how far off I had been. Those steps, wooden and unforgiving, hurt like hell and there was no way I was having sex on them. Ever.

"These steps . . . ummm . . . ouch! Can we, can we stand up, please?"

When we did, my entire body was quivering, and I thought my knees might buckle. While I was trying to regain my senses, Trinity once again took that opportunity to whirl me around and aggressively force me against the door. Unfortunately, my derriere made contact with the handle and a whoosh of air escaped me along with a whimper.

The pain broke the spell and I stood gasping for air, my hand rubbing the injured flesh and my legs widening to steady myself. Keeping my eyes to the floor, I held my other hand out in a way that indicated "stop." Clearly, I needed a minute to get myself together.

Turns out, it didn't take that long and after a few more deep breaths, I whirled around and grabbed the same door handle that had just guaranteed me a wicked bruise. Pulling the door open and without so much as a glance in Trinity's direction, I stumbled towards my car.

But he was quick to follow, and I had no sooner shut and locked the door when Trinity began pounding on the window.

"What's wrong?!" he was saying. "Are you mad at me? What did I do wrong?"

The poor man probably thought he had misread the signals again. The reality was I wasn't running from him, I was trying to escape the unfamiliar and unsettling magnetism between us. Feeling like I needed to set the record straight but unwilling to take a chance that he'd lean in for another disabling kiss, I lowered the electric window a mere inch.

"No, you jerk!" I yelped. "No! Now, I want you!"

With that, I rolled up the window and judging by the look on his face, he was as perplexed as I was. Starting the car, I shifted it into reverse and tore out of his driveway as if the hounds of Hell were at my heels.

On the way home, I was glad that I no longer drove a manual transmission car because if I had, my quaking legs would have made driving nearly impossible. Once home, still trembling over the night's events, I thought of something Trinity had said earlier.

"I'm glad we didn't have sex that first night."

"Based on my M.O.," I'd replied, "it will be a long time before we do."

"Well, I promise that when it does happen, it will be fantastic."

Judging by the chemistry we had just unearthed, I didn't doubt him for a minute.

CHAPTER 14

Days after the tushie-bruising incident, I picked up five gallons of paint and got to work painting a few rooms in Trinity's house while he was at work. Painting was another one of Mom's "do not do this" directives, but she would say it with a paint roller in hand and splatter on her clothes. After my divorce I was looking for ways to bring in income and one of my besties' husbands owned a painting business. He needed help and asked if I'd like to earn a buck, to which I responded I most definitely would. I would serve as his on-call apprentice for almost four years.

I started with prep and cleanup work, but quickly outgrew that role and became more valuable in another. His "graduation" gift to me was an expensive brush. With that, and a good roller pad, he taught me, among other things, how to cut in and the need for quality paint. He kept me busy and when I would return home, exhausted and sore, my mom's words would come back to me and I understood her reason for saying them.

Given my love for task-oriented jobs I often lost track of time, but on the days Trinity had Ian I was mindful to be gone prior to the agreed upon five o'clock deadline. This worked well until one evening when he came home early. Through the garage door bounded an exuberant four-year-old boy who had ginger-colored hair and light brown eyes that were alive with mischief and laughter. His beautiful face was peppered with freckles and his wide, open smile was infectious.

Not having much experience with kids his age I wasn't sure how to relate, but I smiled and greeted him from atop my perch. He, in tiny blue jeans and matching jacket, ran to the ladder and looked up at me, all youthful innocence and chapped red-rimmed lips. I realized then how much his face resembled his dad's; I also took heart that his friendly expression seemed to hold the promise that he was open to having me in his life.

Tonight was not the night to begin that journey, however, and I began tidying up the workspace. I soon abandoned this idea and began balling up used masking tape and throwing it at him, eliciting giggles from both of us. Then, when I was ready to leave, Ian hugged my leg and sat on my foot, begging me to stay. His request was tempting but I knew Trinity treasured his nights with his son and didn't want to intrude. Looking down at Ian's hopeful face, I shook my head and told him we'd meet again. Pressing his face into my leg and hugging it with all his might, he passed gas, causing him to erupt in peals of pure, unadulterated laughter. Trinity and I followed suit. A few minutes later I gently extracted myself and headed out.

Trinity called me after putting Ian to bed. It was the first time we'd spoken at length since the impromptu mashing session.

"I honestly don't know what happened," I said. "I didn't even intend to kiss you and then BOOM! Ground and pound!"

With a chuckle, he said, "Well, you're obviously over thinking of me as a brother; either that or you're a very good actress."

After our conversation ended, I decided it was time to explore the brother connection as well as the strong sense of having known him before. To do so, I turned to meditation, and it didn't disappoint.

I was shown a woman with regal bearing; she wore a high-necked blue silk Victorian dress and her light brown hair was piled ornately on top of her head. After the passing of her parents, the responsibility of caring for both the spacious English estate and her headstrong and impulsive brother was passed down to her.

Standing in the upper-floor library, she heard the whinny of a horse followed by the clatter of hooves. Moving to the four-paned window, she saw her brother whipping his thoroughbred into a gallop. *He's leaving early and in a great hurry, too,* she thought with envy and annoyance. *Probably off on yet another one of his trysts.*

As if sensing his slightly older sister watching, he pivoted his head, his dark hair catching on his handsome face, and flashed her a rakish grin. Then, with one hand gripping the reins and the other still struggling to get through the sleeve of his red frock coat, he managed a wave goodbye.

Returning the wave, she, no stranger to paying off countless gambling and pub debts, consoling ruined maidens and calming their scandalized fathers, sighed and thought, *Please don't create another mess that I'll need to clean up.*

Once out of the meditation, I understood that I was this woman and Trinity was her brother. What I didn't understand and couldn't have known was how greatly those roles would parallel the ones in this lifetime. That night, I was just happy to figure out my previous aversion to kissing Trinity.

A few days later, Trinity invited me over and once there, I shared with him that he had been an irresponsible, scandalous womanizer in the past and I had been his responsible and mature older sister.

"That explains it, then!" he said, laughing.

Though Trinity was not sure about this New Age stuff, he too seemed to like the idea that the mystery had been solved, although I'm sure for different reasons.

I was nervous that given our newly discovered passion, being around each other might be strained. It was an unfounded worry, as the ease – and the laughter - were still there. And when the inevitable kissing began, I would try to cool things down by putting a couch or a kitchen table between us. Of course this was child's play for the former high-school wrestler who still knew how to subdue; yet, despite his considerable skill he didn't go any faster – or any farther - than I was willing to go.

Thanks to the meditation, there was no longer any part of me that felt like he was my brother, and I certainly no longer found his kisses to be horrible; in fact, they were perfect. Even aside from the past life connection, I recognized Trinity was different from others I had dated, yet I couldn't put my finger on what made him unique. He was aggressive, yet gentle and somewhat unsure of himself, and I found all of that to be a potent cocktail.

Eventually we ended our cat and mouse game and wrapped up the evening with another impassioned embrace and seductive kiss. Wanting to sleep in my own bed and knowing I wasn't ready for what it meant to sleep in his, I left. But the joke was on me because once home, there was no sleeping. There were too many questions running through my head and too many hormones racing south of the border.

But the sleepless night was good for something; I made the decision to start on birth control again. I didn't know exactly where we were headed, but given my feelings and his libido, I knew I needed to be ready.

In the days that followed this decision, I started noticing the word "magic" appear with regularity in books, tarot cards, magazines and even a television commercial. As with the recurring threes, it was the frequency that grabbed my attention. But unlike the numbers that had pestered me for months, the significance of this word was easy to figure out: my guardian angels were telling me what I had with Trinity was magic, and I could not argue the truth of this.

Instead, I decided to go with it (or for it, as is the case). After weeks of chatting, flirting and petting, we finally sealed the deal. And, oh my *God* was it steamy, like every smut book I had ever read, and every fantasy I'd had about Trinity, rolled into one off-the-charts experience.

It was days later, while still basking in the afterglow and unable to stop smiling, that I realized we needed to put the brakes on this . . . whatever it was. I know this might seem like a strange choice – it's certainly not a common one - but it was the right one for me. The next time we were together, when things were heating up, I threw a proverbial bucket of cold water on him.

"I *really* wanna hold off on the physical part until we get to know each other better."

His mouth dropped open and whatever had been about to happen was now kiboshed.

Undaunted, I continued, "I need to know you spiritually before I can really give myself to you. Besides, sex is always better when there's feelings involved."

"So, there were no feelings the other night?" he asked with a smirk.

"Nope. Not any emotional or spiritual feelings. Not for me anyway, and until I have those feelings, I'd rather not add the clutter of sex into the mix."

His smirk disappeared.

Admittedly, this was a new approach for me, and judging by the look on his face, it was for him as well. Clearly, he needed more of an explanation and I was happy to continue.

"Based on my past, I need to be able to trust and feel safe before I can entertain a sexual relationship. In order to do this, I need to connect with you on a deeper level; a spiritual level."

At this point I was waiting for the angry response one would expect from a lustful, rejected male. Instead, Trinity took my hand, brought it to his lips and gently kissed it. Then, when his eyes met mine, he told me he would slow things down. I exhaled an emotional breath I had no idea I had been holding.

Unknowingly, I had just taken the first of many steps in changing how I dealt with conflict, and Trinity was instrumental in helping me. In addition, his actions, or lack thereof, were encouraging me to continue. As I drove away that night, and throughout the following weeks, a new song began repeating. It was Don Henley's "The Last Worthless Evening."

Message received, Guys! Thank you.

CHAPTER 15

During one of our marathon phone conversations, Trinity told me that over the years he had attracted some real psychos. For instance, there was the gal who asked him to marry after one week of dating and another who stipulated he must be "on call." Then there was the gal against whom he'd placed a restraining order and yet another who thought the house plans she had glimpsed meant they were reuniting.

And finally, there was the one who broke into his home, snooped in his drawers and poked pinholes in his condoms. She also wrote down two names and phone numbers she saw on the memo pad in his kitchen. One, a female attorney, was a client of Trinity's, and the other was, you guessed it, yours truly.

One evening, as I was making supper, I received a call from a number I didn't recognize. Against my better judgement, I answered.

"Is Trinity there?" some woman asked without any preamble.

"Uh, he doesn't live here," I replied, somewhat confused. I should have said that she had the wrong number, but really it wouldn't have made a difference.

She launched into a spiel about how he had previously done some work for her and this was the number he'd given her. She was concerned because she was trying to fix him up with a friend and he wasn't there to meet them. She wondered if I had seen him or if I knew where he was.

My budding intuition, or as I like to call it my "spidey sense," told me something was not right. The explanation was too long and detailed to be the truth.

"Who is this?"

"Jessica," she replied without hesitation.

Immediately, I *knew* she was lying, and what's more, I felt as if she was pretending to be my niece. Instead of calling her bullshit out, I simply told "Jessica" I couldn't help her and hung up without so much as a goodbye.

Minutes later, another call, and this time from a blocked number. Intrigued, I answered and though the voice was different, I heard the same background noises.

She, too, asked for Trinity, to which I curtly replied, "You have the wrong number."

"Who are you?" she asked with attitude.

"Who I am is none of your damn business."

She then got right to the heart of the matter.

"Are you sleeping with him?! You know he's sleeping with four different women at the same time, right? And you know he gave his ex-wife gonorrhea so bad that she had to have a hysterectomy. He is bad news and we *(we?)* just wanted to warn you about him."

"I appreciate your concern, but I don't need the warning. Goodbye." Hanging up, I shook my head and thought, *Jesus!* Why did I say that?! Because I'm so flippin' "North Dakota Nice," that's why.

I tried not to let her words bother me, but like those of the vile psychic, they crept in anyway. What if it was true? Had he really given his ex-wife a sexually transmitted disease that was so bad she had to have a hysterectomy? He certainly hadn't said anything to me about that. After thinking about it for a few moments, I decided it wasn't true. But sleeping with four other women? That *might* be true, given his history, but it really didn't fit with the sweet, sensitive and sometimes vulnerable man I was getting to know.

With shaking hands, I called Rya. She said I needed to tell Trinity about these phone calls immediately, both for his sake and mine. I knew she was right, but Trinity was playing in a poker tournament and was away from his phone. I preferred to speak with him directly, but since I didn't know how long he'd be out of touch I left a detailed message and instantly felt better.

That feeling didn't last long. Two hours later, my phone came to life again, only it wasn't Trinity calling; it was a blocked number. Not eager for another round of captivating conversation, I didn't answer. A few minutes passed, then another call and this time, they left a message. I didn't want to listen to their ramblings but was afraid not to, so, with my heart pounding, I pressed the play button.

The message was from the person who had previously identified herself as "Jessica," and she was very drunk.

"I've been seeing Trinity for four months," she slurred. "He did horrible things to his ex-wife and she needed to be made whole again by having a hysterectomy. You are nothing but a slut and a whore who is hanging out with a pathetic alcoholic and a crippled veteran."

My mouth fell open in surprise. *What the hell?* I'm a slut and a whore? They don't even know me. How did these lulus get my number anyway? And if they have that, do they also know where I live? I stood rooted to my spot as these thoughts, as well as others, ran through my mind. Fearing for my safety, I called the non-emergency police line, then, as the anxiety-inducing paralysis wore off, I double-checked the locks on my door and windows. But even with those precautions I was unable to relax and, needless to say, I did not sleep well.

Early the next morning, Trinity called and apologized for not getting back to me the previous night. His tournament ran late and he hadn't brought his phone because they were prohibited. By the time he got home and checked his messages, it was well past three. He went on to say that he had received several abusive messages, as had a female client of his. As I updated him on the message from my answering machine, he began noticing things were displaced in his home. He would talk to me soon, he said, but right now he had to call the police.

When they arrived, it was immediately determined that the lock to the front door was broken. After dusting for fingerprints and listening to his messages, Trinity told the police he thought he knew who the culprit was: an obsessed neighbor from his past. He then told them this woman swore he was the father of her child even though he had never slept with her and to prove it, he had voluntarily taken a paternity test.

As it turned out, Trinity's finger-pointing was spot on. The police investigated and found this woman had a long history of stalking not only Trinity but others as well. They also found emails and records of the slanderous phone calls to me, Trinity and his client.

I was relieved when Trinity said he was pressing charges; I also told him that if he hadn't, I would have.

And with that, another conflict-nullifying step was taken; Miss Don't Make Waves was on a roll.

CHAPTER 16

Even from that tense situation, beauty appeared. The week following the harassing phone calls was especially busy for both of us, but we carved out time for each other, be it a quick lunch, or long, candid phone calls. And during the quiet moments, I would reflect on how I had unfairly judged this book by its cover only to find, upon taking a second look, that the story inside was worth reading. With that realization came another: I was in love and I knew he was too. Unlike me, however, he was nowhere near ready to acknowledge it.

I had studied this sensitive, smart, and sometimes insecure man with eyes wide open. Not wanting a repeat of my marriage, I was aware of what I viewed as potential pitfalls, but those would be discussed – and worked through – as we moved forward. First though, I wanted to show him I wholeheartedly loved him, and I did just that the next time we were alone. Instead of putting the brakes on when things got going, I gave myself to him, heart and soul. And while our first time, some weeks earlier, was earth-shattering, this time it was indescribable, proving that sex really *is* better when there are feelings involved.

As they say, old habits die hard, and unfortunately I had some habits, actually, one in particular, that kept me from enjoying our love-making to the fullest. What I am talking about is a lifetime of faking orgasms, a pattern I now carried into my relationship with Trinity.

Instantly regretting my dishonesty, I realized this wasn't how I wanted to start this aspect of our relationship. We both deserved better, I felt, and I needed to tell him what I had done along with the history behind it. Just the thought of having that conversation was enough to make me squirm, but in the end my desire to set things right with him outweighed my discomfort. I told him it didn't feel right to lie to him and, true to form, Trinity said he wouldn't accept anything less than authentic.

Without knowing it, he was teaching me that I shouldn't either.

CHAPTER 17

In between engrossing conversations and romps in the hay, I continued painting Trinity's glaringly white walls. After finishing the living and dining rooms as well as the kitchen, I decided it was time for his bedroom. I chose a burnt pumpkin color, and after much debate, I succeeded in convincing Trinity it would be beautiful. Now I needed to prove it.

When Trinity came home, he opened a bottle of wine and ordered us some food. Then, holding a wine glass, he walked into the bedroom where he casually leaned against the door jamb and looked at me with appreciation. His hazel-green eyes told me all I needed to know: he liked having life in his home when he returned from work; he was as attracted to me as I was to him; and, he loved me.

Climbing down the ladder, I walked to him, arms out, and fluidly fell into his for a hug. We shared a tender kiss and then snuggled into each other's embrace again.

"I thought your color choice was insane," he said, "but now that I see it, I really like it!"

"Oh my gosh! I'm so glad to hear that!" I replied, silently adding, *Told ya so*!

Then, walking hand in hand, we went to the kitchen where a glass of wine was waiting for me. While we sipped, we chatted about our day and then he decided to divulge a secret.

"I have a confession to make. Did I ever tell you how insecure and nervous I was that night we first had sex?"

"What?!"

"Yeah, I really wanted to please you. I was kinda feeling like I'd fail you in some way. I think I was a little intimidated that you're older than me."

"What does my *age* have to do . . . *You're* the one who was a complete whore!"

"I guess what I'm trying to say is that I wanted to erase everyone else from your mind. I wanted it to be like it was your first time and I wanted it to be special."

Aww.

I was still feeling all warm and fuzzy when the delivery guy arrived with our food. As we were sitting down to eat, his house phone rang, but he let it go to voicemail and we continued our discussion. There was no shortage of things to talk about and we found ourselves giggling over the silliest of them. As good friends and lovers often do, we were starting to develop our own language, and making some real memories.

When supper was finished I, the diligent taskmaster, cleared the table before returning to the semi-painted bedroom. Trinity went to check his voicemail and returned a couple of moments later wearing a perplexed look. He cocked his head and unconsciously scratched an imaginary itch by his mouth. His brows were drawn inward, and his lips formed a quizzical half-smile.

"Well, that was weird. I just got a message from a girl I used to date in high school. I wonder what that's all about."

Suddenly, time appeared to move in slow motion. I missed my next inhalation and my eyes momentarily widened into an unblinking stare. I felt the icy fingers of panic grip my heart. Trying to dismiss this foreboding feeling, I pretended it wasn't real. *Ignore it and it will go away,* I told myself, but deep down I knew something wicked this way would come.

A heartbeat later, time resumed, as did my breath. I smiled, acting as if nothing was wrong, while shrugging my shoulders in an attempt to shake off these unsettling feelings. Then, with the cold seeping from my chest into my stomach, I picked up a paint brush, kissed Trinity's cheek, and walked to his bedroom.

I was unable to concentrate, however, and as the work demanded attention to detail, I decided to call it a night. Trinity, noticing a change in my disposition, asked what was wrong. Unsure of how much to tell him, I opted to say nothing. I would later wonder whether it would have changed anything had I just been forthcoming. Instead, I mumbled that I wasn't feeling well, which was true enough but had nothing to do with food, drink, or paint fumes. He tried to convince me to stay, but I needed some space, a decision I would also regret because nothing was the same after that.

This instantaneous knowing, and subsequent ignoring, wasn't new to me. There had been at least two previous instances where the Guys had tried to warn me that something catastrophic was on the horizon.

The first time, I was in a bar, laughing, drinking and yell-talking with my best friend. For over a year, we'd been nearly inseparable. We regularly had homemade Sunday suppers with her mom and she was my companion on each trip to Minot. Where one of us was, the other was sure to follow.

After a few cocktails, my friend announced she needed a bathroom break. As I waited for her to return, I stood near the dance floor, smiling as I watched the throngs of uninhibited people gyrating to the blaring beat of the music.

Suddenly, the multicolored strobe lights and the din of the music began to fade, and my body felt immobile, like a heavy statue. Swiveling my eyes around the bar, I thought, *What's going on here? No one else appears to be affected.*

Then, a low humming noise began inside my head, and I felt as if I had entered a sensory deprivation chamber. As the intensity level rose, time seemed to slow down. The dance floor's bright colors had faded to grayscale, the music sounded far away, and the smell of perfume, alcohol and sweat had disappeared.

Inside my head, a deep masculine voice ominously warned, *She will betray you.*

With those words, the buffering dissolved. My senses immediately returned, as did the sounds, lights and smells of the bar. My smile faltered as my startled eyes sought my bestie. She was talking to someone, her head thrown back in laughter, and when she saw me looking, she waved and offered a little smile.

Fuck! No. NOOOOOO! Don't let this be true! I thought. Then, knowing it would happen, I added with a visible shrug, *Well, let's have some fun before it ends.*

Her betrayal happened shortly thereafter, forever severing our friendship.

The second warning hit even closer to home, because this time it was about my beloved mother. During my adulthood, Mom had always been very social, physically active and young at heart; however, in recent years her quality of life had drastically declined due to high blood pressure, smoking and heart disease. When her cardiovascular problem progressed to the point where she could barely walk without becoming winded, her doctor recommended she have heart valve replacement surgery, a procedure, he said, that was routine nowadays and not a cause for concern.

This was back when I was married to Ben, and Mom and Dad decided to spend a few days with us in our newly built home before continuing on to St. Paul, where the surgery was taking place. As Dad was backing their Cadillac out of our driveway, I distractedly waved goodbye to them. Mom looked at me through the tinted passenger side window and I was struck with the knowledge she wouldn't be returning. Like a clap of thunder, this knowing reverberated throughout my mind.

Stunned, I dropped my eyes and stared unseeingly at our garage floor. *This is crazy,* I thought. *Mom's not gonna die.* Once again, time seemed to have slowed down. I shook my head as if to rid myself of the thought. When I returned my gaze to the car, I saw that she was smiling tenderly.

Taking in her face, I noticed her smile, eyes, and countenance were all saying goodbye. And when she maintained eye contact a little bit longer than was sufficient, I knew *she* also knew this was a one-way trip. Time returned to normal when the car accelerated, and she gave me an off-handed wave. Shrugging, I told myself it was just nerves or an overactive imagination. Truth is, I didn't want it to be true and thought if I ignored it then maybe it wouldn't be.

The next day, my husband and I drove to St. Paul. My mom had made it through surgery but was in a medically induced coma due to complications. As Ben and I lay sleeping in our king-sized hotel bed, I heard my name. Waking up, and without moving, I looked around the darkened bedroom. I was just beginning my spiritual growth in 1999, but I *knew* my mom had called to me; I also knew that she had died.

But she was with me now. I felt her floating above me and her energy caress my cheek. I knew my mom was saying goodbye and I was overwhelmed with gratitude for the awareness of it. Then I felt a crushing weight push me into the mattress. I could not move a muscle, but it was not painful or frightening. As my body was being pushed deeper into the plush pillow top by an unseen force, I heard several bedsprings groan in protest. A sense of acceptance and tranquility flowed through me while, next to me, my husband continued to snore.

I told myself that maybe I was wrong, maybe Mom was still alive. I was innately trying to protect myself from the blinding agony I sensed was coming. Staring at the ceiling, a tear escaped and slowly rolled into my hair. Mom's energy was gone now but I could still feel the comfort it provided. Knowing the phone would soon ring, I continued to pretend she was alive.

When the portended call came, it shattered my make-believe world. My husband, instantly awake, bolted upright and fumbled for the phone. The caller said we needed to get to the hospital quickly, as there had been a new development. Ben hung up and hastily rolled over to wake me.

Already knowing what he was about to say, with a wistful smile and in a voice that was full of certainty, I said, "She's dead. My mom is dead."

"You don't know that!" he exclaimed. "Get *up*! Let's go!"

He sprinted toward the bathroom and I thought, *I've never seen him move so fast!* In fact, if the situation wasn't so dire, I might have laughed at his absurdity.

As it was, I remained in bed and quietly repeated, "There's no reason to rush. She's gone."

With that, the paralysis left my body and I was resting on top of the mattress once again. I sat up, letting the covers fall off me. Taking in a deep breath, I dropped my head backwards, closed my eyes and exhaled. My body was saying, *Let's face this. Let's move through it.* But my mind wasn't ready.

After adjusting my head so that it sat on top of my neck, I swung my legs out of bed, feeling the Berber carpet as I placed my hands on either side of my hips. Leaning forward, I slowly pushed myself off the bed and dressed in a state of shock, not caring what I wore. My mind kept returning to the feeling of energetic oneness I had felt with my mom as she left the physical plane and I kept thinking about how elated and effervescent that had allowed me to feel.

Once in the car, Ben broke all the posted speed limits; he also kept glancing at me and asking if I was okay. I remained eerily calm, almost passive as I repeated that he needed to slow down or there were going to be at least two more people dying that night. With that, he let his eyes linger on my profile and out of the corner of my eye I could see genuine concern on his face. I couldn't tell, though, whether he was worried about my mental health or that we would arrive too late.

My dad, having stayed closer to the hospital, had arrived moments before us. He waited at the ICU entryway and his countenance triggered powerful and traumatic memories. When I was a child, my mom had been in and out of hospitals. I was left in the waiting rooms where I would anxiously watch people come and go. I noticed how they silently filled Styrofoam cups with black coffee and how they would pace or read magazines. Then, when I'd had enough of that, I'd look at the television without seeing or hearing it.

Afraid I would not be there when my dad came for me, I never wanted to use the bathroom or go to the cafeteria. Instead, to keep myself occupied, I would often color, play silent games, or use my imagination to weave stories about others. Sometimes I would sit cross-legged with a rounded back on the cold polished quartz floor only a few feet in front of the elevator doors. Other times, I would rest on uncomfortable padless chairs. Regardless of where I sat or what I did, I kept an impatient and vigilant eye out for my dad. His presence meant it was my turn to see Mom, and in seeing her, all the fears my mind created would disappear.

Now, I silently walked past my dad, then the nurses' station, noting their looks of surprise as I did so. I had this thought that I shouldn't be doing this, yet I continued to steamroll towards the room where, just hours earlier, I had held my mom's hand, massaged her feet and whispered that I loved her.

While doing this, I had noticed she had felt warm to the touch, and when I told the nurse Mom didn't like to be that warm, she smiled and took some blankets off her. She told me that even in her comatose state, Mom could hear me. This brought me comfort because as long as I could remember, I had been her self-appointed guardian and caretaker. The reason for this was self-preservation; as a child I feared she was going to die and if she did, who would take care of me?

Sometimes this fear would take me to my parents' bedroom where I would listen for the sound of her breathing. If it was faint, I would poke her and if she grunted or turned over, I was satisfied. Then, more often than not, I would either climb into their bed, finding a space between the two of them or curl my tiny body into a ball and sleep blanketless on the carpeted floor next to her.

As Ben sat in a chair, I found myself wishing he wasn't there so I could talk with her privately. Along with other things, I wanted to proclaim that I, her faithful protector, was keeping an unfailing watch over her and that she was doing beautifully. But mostly, I wanted to lay with her, arms draped loosely around her, and listen to her breathe.

But I did none of those things because I wasn't comfortable asking my husband to leave. That would be a bitter lesson learned.

Now my worst childhood fear had happened, and as I neared her hospital room my cadence was slowed by a vision of bright red blood all over her face and neck and the floor. Just then, a nurse rounded the corner, and knowing I shouldn't see what awaited, he reached his arms wide. It was that motion that effectively halted my shock walk and confirmed my earlier thought; she was gone. My eyes met his and with tenderness, he asked if I was here to see my mom. I couldn't find my voice, so I simply nodded. With that, tears filled my eyes, spilled over, and my calm facade cracked.

"We are taking good care of her," he said while maintaining eye contact, "but she's not ready to be seen yet. We still have to finish cleaning her up. How about you come with me and wait in this room with the rest of your family? A doctor will be in shortly."

I mindlessly nodded and allowed him to usher me into a conference room where my dad was waiting. Instead of going to him, I stood where I was; Dad wasn't the consoling kind.

"Melissa," he said after the doctor had delivered the news and left, "you'd better call your brother and let him know. When you're done, I'll call your sister."

Relieved to be given a task, I nodded obediently and reached for the phone.

My brother lived in a different time zone, where it was one hour earlier. I didn't think about that, though; I just wanted to complete the job and let Dad do his.

When he answered, he made a joke, his attempt at avoiding the inevitable, and I immediately understood that he knew why his phone was ringing at an ungodly hour. Perhaps I should have made small talk, let him believe our mom was alive for just a bit longer, but in a rush to complete what my dad had asked of me, I blurted, "Bruce. Mom is dead."

With that short utterance, I knew his life had been changed forever, just as all of ours had. We had lost our mother at the young age of seventy-two, and Dad lost his wife of fifty-two years.

CHAPTER 18

As I said earlier, I had discovered - or uncovered - a lot of things about Trinity, many I loved, others that I didn't care for. One example was his strong dislike for authority figures; this rough and tough Army Ranger didn't like being told what to do. When I asked how that worked out in the military, he replied that it hadn't. He smirked and said the countless pushups he'd had to do made him stronger.

Trinity was also stubborn. And when I say stubborn, I do not mean *tenacious, persistent,* or *determined.* I mean *headstrong* and *pigheaded,* characteristics that often worked to his disadvantage. In addition, he also had some deep-seated self-worth issues, which he deflected with sarcastic, demeaning comments like, "All girls cheat, it's just a matter of time."

I knew I was in well over my head with this defiant, full-blooded German man. Yet, despite that, he was the one I had been dreaming of and yearning for. He was the one who fit my written description detailing what I wanted in a forever husband. He was the one I wanted to have children with and to grow old alongside. He demanded I see my beauty and to feel beautiful; he encouraged me to be strong and face my fears. With equal parts passion and tenderness, he was a very enchanting package.

When I was with him, I felt complete and no longer wondered when my life would begin or when I would find my soulmate. He had awoken something slumbering inside of me and, at the same time, stole the breath from my body. Without a doubt, I would wholeheartedly give my life for him and yet I wanted to be with him forever. He was my Other, my true love, the "One," and I knew I was the same to him. Too bad I, or the emotions he was feeling about me, caused him to panic.

Within six weeks of the ex-girlfriend's message, my sense of foreboding was proven accurate when he unceremoniously dumped me.

CHAPTER 19

It was a sunny April afternoon, the kind of beautiful day that stands out in stark relief from the harshness of winter. For the second time in less than a week, I found myself engaging in another awkward phone conversation with Trinity, filled with lengthy pauses and superficial banter. Not willing to waste my time indoors, I told him I needed to go. This was the catalyst he needed.

"Melissa? I don't know if this is right," he choked out. "I . . . I don't know if I'm screwing things up, but I have to try. I've been talking with my ex-girlfriend and I wanna try things with her again."

Then, after another long delay, he got down to business. "I need to break up with you."

And there it is.

Outwardly, I remained calm, just as I had that night long ago when I saw my husband being groped in a bar. But, also like that night, I was seething internally. My mind screamed, WHAT?! WHAT THE FUCK?! *You're breaking up with me?* ME?!

Trinity had once commented that he thought I might be a great actress. Now, in a truly Oscar-worthy performance, I proved him right. "I deeply care for you," I replied without a trace of the anguish I was feeling, "but I completely understand. You have to do what you have to do." I almost added, *I'll be here for you when you're ready,* but my brain yelled, STOP! *Don't you dare!*

When he disconnected, I stared in disbelief at the phone. Stunned, I blinked my eyelids in rapid succession and thought, *Umm, what the hell just happened? Did he just dump me for an ex-lover? Yeah, I think he did. Well, what about all those things he said, like wanting to be a better person and that I calmed him? And what about the plans we made for the summer? And the sex, the mind-blowing sex for God's sake, how could he give that up? How could he give all this up for a relationship that hadn't worked in the first place?!*

Trying to make sense out of this, I sat in my computer chair, numb with shock, mouth open and eyes staring. I remained this way for several minutes until the phone reminded me with a shrill, irritating noise, that I hadn't hung up.

Doing so, I turned my thoughts to the now validated feelings of the past few weeks. I'd felt him pulling away but chalked it up to him being busier than usual at work. Days would go by without him calling or returning my messages. And when he did call, he had excuses as to why we couldn't get together. On the rare evenings we did, he was often distracted and spoke cryptically.

One night, as we were watching a television drama, he teasingly said, "Oh no! The world is about to end! What should we do?!"

Thinking we should come clean about loving each other, I smiled and said, "We should tell each other all of our secrets!"

"Oh," he replied, "there might be a thing or two I'd like to tell you."

I didn't hear anything but love coming from that sentence; it felt as if we were of the same mind. However, as I revisited that memory, I saw things differently.

I also replayed a snippet of a conversation I'd recently had with Jessica.

"Do you think he's cheating on you?" she asked.

Thinking this was the most ridiculous thing I had ever heard, I said, "What? No way. He's not like that."

Now I wasn't so sure.

Even through my haze, I knew what I needed to do; I needed to tell Rya and Susie. Not ready for a phone conversation, I raised my hands to the keyboard and began composing an email to Susie. As I did, a few warm tears leaked from my eyes. Letting them fall, I sent the email and allowed my heavy arms to drop into my lap. My eyes unfocused as my mind resumed its endless questioning. Shouldn't I be crying? Isn't that the norm when someone you love dumps you? *Why am I not crying?* These thoughts tumbled over and over until Susie's email notification broke the loop.

"Breathe, Missy Pooh," she wrote. "It looks like he's looking down two roads and wants to make sure he picks the right one. But all is not lost. It looks like if you can walk confidently down your path for a while, he'll walk down this one and he'll see it's not for him. Actually, it looks like he won't even get to walk down the path. Either she'll say no right away, or he'll take one look at the relationship and say, 'Oh, now I remember why we didn't stay together.' There's unfinished business with her and it looks like he doesn't want to have regrets."

Susie had never failed to comfort or uplift me, and that day was no different. Her words flowed through me with love and compassion, and after reading them for the second time, the shock began to fade. And as it did, my body shuddered and the tears came, an ocean of them. So much so that I wondered if they were ever going to stop.

Hours later, when the torrent had weakened to a trickle, I turned to my tarot cards. After asking about my current situation, I shuffled the deck and turned over one card. Disbelieving, I repeated this action, and again, the same card was drawn. Ever the one to want or, more accurately, *demand* more signs, I performed this process for the third time, and was met with the same answer. Thinking I understood the message but wanting to be sure, I read the notes on the "Laughter" card. I was being asked to infuse laughter into this situation and trust that there will be a silver lining.

Buoyed by this, I decided to ask one more question. After shuffling the deck, I asked if Trinity would return within two to three months, and then drew one card: Romantic Partner. Feeling as if this confirmed what Susie had said and what I felt, additional validation was not needed, and I put the deck away.

Until his return, I would do what I could to work through the grief. In order to do that, though, I needed to go within and be alone. Rya would invite me places but I would decline. Instead I went for solitary walks, meditated, deepened my spiritual practice and lived at the gym. But perhaps most importantly, I focused on what I could control, which, thankfully, wasn't much.

At one point, when the grief threatened to turn into depression, I, like a petulant child, asked my guardian angels to kick Trinity's ass. Without delay, I heard, *It is done* and while I knew they would do nothing of the sort and were merely consoling me, I thought, *Thanks for having my back, Guys.*

Shortly after that, I dreamt of a puppy with large, soulful brown eyes that were filled with immeasurable pain. Once awake, I thought this was me but then, in a flash, I knew it was Trinity. I also knew this had nothing to do with my wish; Trinity had done this to himself and, in all honesty, a part of me hoped he was in pain over losing me.

About three months after Trinity left me, I heard through the grapevine (the "grapevine" being Jessica) that it hadn't worked out with Trinity's ex-girlfriend. Apparently, she hadn't wanted to rekindle their romance and shut him down as soon as he brought it up, just as Susie predicted.

Nice to see you're still misreading those signals, Trinity.

This brought a satisfied half-smile to my face, but Jessica's next words removed it. She said he, after meeting someone new, had sold his house, found a job and moved to Mankato, Minnesota, where they were now living together.

What?! The blood drained from my face. He *moved*? He's *living* with a *girl*?! How could that even happen when he was supposed to return to me as soon as he had tied up the loose "ex-girlfriend" ends? I had felt so strongly about that and now, with this new development, I knew his absence would be much longer, if not forever. *Dammit!*

This was a blow I had not seen coming and the progress I had made mending my broken heart was erased. I became angry; didn't Trinity know he loved me and that I was waiting for him? I was also upset with the Guys since they had validated a short time span. Ultimately, I ended up hoping I would at least learn why this had happened; until then, the only choice was to continue my journey.

I didn't have to wait long to understand how far I had already come. Once the news spread, a few friends and relatives tried to offer their support by trash-talking Trinity.

"This is not helpful," I said, surprising myself, for I used to do the same thing. "Trinity's following his own guidance and trying to resolve old issues. Having you belittle him is not okay. Yes, I'm devastated by his decision, but he's trying to better himself. Who are we to judge?"

Not only was I using my voice, but, in that moment, I began teaching with it.

Susie and Rya were sources of strength and with each check-in they reassured me, each in her own unique way, that I was loved and would get through this. The encouragement from these "sisters from another mother" helped, but something more was needed. I was almost finished with Reiki training and my intuitive abilities had grown exponentially. Because of this, I knew I needed to make a trip home and see my dad. I did so without delay.

As I was falling asleep in the downstairs guest bedroom, I thought of Trinity. An internal voice said, *He loves you,* and before I had a chance to question this, the voice repeated, *He loves you, he loves you, he loves you.* With a sigh, I asked if Trinity was coming back to me. *No. He is lost.*

Even though this validated my knowing, it was still painful to hear, and ever-present tears formed as the voice repeated, *He loves you.*

"A lot of good that does me," I replied through tears. "Will you Guys do me a favor, please? Tomorrow, each time he is thinking about me, will you show me the color orange?" Not hearing, nor expecting a reply, I closed my eyes and attempted sleep.

Their answer came the next day, though, loud and clear. Without seeking it, and everywhere I looked, there was orange. I had to hand it to the Guys, they had really brought their A game.

Loving the confirmation but wanting more, I thought, *Show me his name. Please.* Then, intending to check emails, I sat down at Dad's computer desk and there, on the keyboard, was a bill from *Trinity* Hospital. Afraid it was an illusion, I touched it and then, despite my broken heart, I couldn't help but smile.

More affirmation was provided on Sunday when I was packing to return to Fargo. Randomly singing Rob Thomas' "Lonely No More," a tune which repeated itself even after waving goodbye, I turned on my car's stereo and listened as that song floated out of the speakers.

Smiling once again, I figured out why I needed to make the trip; it had given me an answer to a previously asked, but unanswered, question. We are never alone; angels surround us constantly. And, as was the case with me, they are willing to play silly color games and have items seemingly materialize out of thin air in order to prove it.

From that day forward, my trust in the unseen grew.

Months later, my mom would deliver an important message. I was still grappling with heartache, and my thoughts often turned to Trinity; I wondered if he was well, and why he hadn't returned to me.

In a dream, Mom and I were on a golf course during the quiet and beauty of the early dawn hours. The sun was peeking through a light mist and as I stood in the trees, just off the fairway, she, in full golf regalia, walked towards me.

He's afraid of you, she said.

I shook my head as if I hadn't heard her correctly. *What?*

Not bothering to look at me or slow her pace, she continued past me. *He's afraid of the depth of his emotions for you. He's afraid of how much he cares.*

I stared at her back and my mouth fell open. *Mom! I miss you and I love you! I have so many questions. Can you stay?*

She gave me her answer by continuing her stroll to the sun-dappled green.

I was still thinking about the dream a few days later as I drove along an unfamiliar road while running errands. At a stop light, I noticed the car's license plate in front of me was "DUH 333."

Et tu Brute? I thought as an ache stabbed my heart.

But when I returned home, my caller ID showed a missed call from Trinity, and the blinking answering machine light showed I had a message. Immediately, my pulse increased and my mouth went dry. Was this what I had been hoping for and dreaming of? *Please God, please God,* PLEASE *let it be!*

Unable to wait another second, I jabbed the recorder's play button and let out an excited squeal. The speaker came alive with his beautiful voice and a smile parted my face. It was soon replaced by a frown because he wasn't calling to reconcile or even apologize; he was calling to tell me he appreciated all the hard work I had done painting his home. He went on to say he didn't understand how much work it was until he had to do some painting himself. He finished by saying, almost as an afterthought, that I could call him to chat . . . if I wanted.

What the ever-loving shit? Confused and crushed, my scowl deepened as outrage boiled to the surface. I could call him to "*chat*" like we were old friends and he hadn't broken my heart into a thousand pieces? Then, with a flash of clarity, I understood why he *really* called; he wanted sex.

That awareness ignited an explosive firestorm of rage. I vented my indignation to a quiet apartment. "A BOOTY CALL! That *fucker* thinks he can booty call *me*?! After what we *had*?! No *fucking* way! NO FUCKING WAY!" Oh, hell no. This was *not* happening. "That's what I am to you now, huh? Just a casual *fuck*?!" Then, with all the rancor I could muster, I stomped my foot and screamed, "GO FUCK YOURSELF!"

Instead of immediately returning his call, I wisely decided to apply the 24-Hour Rule, which meant I would sit with this for a full twenty-four hours before acting upon it. Hopefully, that would be enough time to calm my chapped ass down and to determine how I wanted, *if* I wanted, to handle this. As it turns out, the 24-Hour Rule lasted three weeks and I needed every minute of that time to chill the eff out.

After golfing with the girls and drinking some liquid courage, I returned home and decided it was now or never. In order to encourage the return of my powerful emotions, I thought of what he said and how I felt because of it. Within seconds, I had a head full of steam and the words "You motherfucker" on the tip of my tongue. I then dialed his number. Listening to it ring, something unexpected happened; I felt fear and realized I didn't want to talk to him.

To my credit, though, I didn't hang up; instead I prayed for his voicemail. After four rings, my prayers were answered and as I suspected, his voice caused me to wince and my anger faltered. *Maybe this isn't such a good idea*, I thought, but by then his narrative had ended and I heard the beep. *Here we go,* I thought as I sucked in a deep breath, and in short, clipped tones said, "No thank you! No! You may *not* booty call me. *Ever!!* I deserve better than that. Do *not* contact me again unless you're willing to be honest with yourself and with me."

Mic drop.

CHAPTER 20

Months after that, Rya served as both the voice of truth and encouragement. While I remained steadfast in my belief that Trinity would someday return, she gently advocated for me to expand my dating horizons, and even suggested I go online. I told her that while that didn't hold any allure for me, I'd try to keep an open mind. After a few more months without any word from Trinity, my hope faded, and I reluctantly agreed with her. Considering it had been almost eighteen months since he threw us away, I needed to do what he had and move on.

Shutting that door lessened the constriction I felt when I saw his picture in the newspaper weeks later. Reading the caption below it, I learned he was once again living in Fargo and working for a different company. Staring at the image longer than I should have, I noticed it no longer caused searing pain but rather a wistful sadness. And then, after tracing his face with my fingertip, I silently wished him well and turned the page.

Unbeknownst to me, Trinity had occasionally updated Jessica on what was happening in his life, specifically things like it hadn't worked out with the gal, or the job, in Mankato. His aim, of course, was for Jessica to relay the information to me and in turn share some of my intel with him. He couldn't have known that she saw, firsthand, the devastation he had caused, and possibly he forgot that she was born into a family that rarely lets go of grudges.

Because of that, when Trinity started sniffing around, she became very protective. She even employed a bit of misdirection, telling him she thought I was seeing someone. When I found out about this, I told her I appreciated her efforts, but I wasn't comfortable with that lie. I also let her know I didn't want protection; I wanted fate to move forward.

Maybe that's why I started seeing threes everywhere again, but this time, instead of eliciting excitement, they caused apprehension. I was still miffed at the Guys for their perceived timeframe betrayal. I had yet to learn that they had absolutely nothing to do with it; that was all Trinity's doing. Because we have free will, we can, and often do, deviate from the preset plan.

If, for instance, after Trinity found his ex-girlfriend didn't want to reunite, he could have closed the lesson book and returned, as is, to me. If he had done that, the roughly predicted two-to-three-month time span would have been accurate. But some part of Trinity understood that he could further his emotional healing by continuing his learning journey and reconnecting with me when he had less encumbrances. This meant he would need to be gone longer, but the rewards would be greater, for both of us. A risky proposition, for sure, and one without guarantees; nevertheless, he opted to do so which, in turn, took him to another city and another girl.

But it wasn't just Trinity who was benefiting from the time apart. I was in a much better place too, in part due to a woman I had met on the golf course while she and I were both married. What began as a casual friendship grew stronger after her divorce when she became my neighbor. Over scotcheroo bars and hallway conversations, she invited me to family gatherings. Then, during the summer months, she started regularly asking me to the lake house she shared with her siblings. It was there that I found what had eluded me in the city: freedom from my thoughts.

The lake house was filled with unconditional acceptance, abundant laughter, and caring words. At night, there were bonfires where we watched shooting stars, and pontoon rides where I learned how to pee without getting in the water.

These people, whom have since become family to me, made it the perfect haven in which to heal. With a roof over my head, food in my belly and the troubles of Fargo briefly forgotten, I closely watched their dynamics and soon decided my next relationship would be modeled after them. It was clear that even after years of marriage and raising children, these spouses were still both *in* love and loved.

The drives there consisted of open windows and belting out my heartbreak to Kelly Clarkson's "Behind These Hazel Eyes" and Christina Aguilera's "Fighter." The return trips were often silent and filled with contentment.

If Trinity was still in my life, I might not have discovered this amazing group, nor would I have been blessed with so many wonderful memories.

I was still feeling the cumulative effects of a summer's worth of lake time when, on a warm September evening, the phone rang. This time caller ID was not needed; I knew who was calling. As I mentally prepared, I drew in a breath and casually reached for the phone.

"Hi Trinity," I said, my voice cool but pleasant. "It's nice to hear from you. Why are you calling?"

"Hi, Melissa. I just wanna talk."

"Okay," I said. "Talk."

Without hesitation, Trinity started talking, and it was everything I had been dreaming he'd say. Breaking up with me was the stupidest thing he had ever done, and he knew it the second he'd hung up the phone that day. He felt like he'd lost the best thing that ever happened to him and he had wanted to call me for well over a year (my angels were right!) but then decided he had things to do before he made that call. And finally, he thanked me because he had done a lot of learning, and a lot of growing up.

I was just as open with him. First, I announced that I'd known he'd call again because we had unfinished business. Then I told him I could tell by the way he'd broken up with me that he was not completely sure about his decision.

"About that," he said. "Why did you just let me go? I mean, you didn't even fight for me."

To me, it was common sense. "Why would I want to persuade someone to stay when they've made it clear they want to be with someone else?"

"Ooooh," he said, understanding. "Nobody's done that before. They've all whined or gotten mad. You were so classy and that cemented a place in my heart for you."

"Then why did you really break up with me?"

"Our relationship was just so perfect, and I don't have a good track record with things that I love. I kept waiting for the crash and when that didn't happen, I looked for a way out."

Well, you found it.

"Why are you calling me now, after all this time?"

What he said next truly blew my mind.

"I received a random email about a month ago that dropped me to my knees. I normally don't read stuff like that, but for some reason this time I did. It said, '*If you leave the one you love for the one you like, the one you like will leave you for the one they love.*'"

My mouth dropped. Not only was he telling me he loved me, albeit in a roundabout way, he was also confirming the craftiness of the Universe. I was floored that such a perfect message had mimicked everything I felt.

Just as I was thinking it couldn't get any better, Trinity proved me wrong.

"I've missed you," he continued. "Your personality, positivity, straightforwardness and your weird ability to calm me. I thought of you constantly, even when I was living with someone (the color orange!). I wondered what you were doing, who you were with, if you ever thought of me and if I had missed my chance. There's just something about you, I can't put my finger on it, but you're different from all the rest."

Got that right, bucko.

If this was a romance novel, I would have fallen into his arms, his considerable crimes forgiven. But this was no romance novel, and while everything he said was pleasing to the ears, the reality was he had broken my heart, then added insult to injury by calling me to shag months later. He obviously thought that I was going to fall all over myself to be with him again, but he was sadly mistaken.

As he said, I was different than the rest.

When I asked him about the lame "just wanted to thank you" message, he swore it was not meant as a booty call, but that he had genuinely taken for granted all the hard work I had done.

Letting dead air hang between us for a second or two, I scoffed, "Utter bullshit."

"Yeah, well, it was more of a *pulse check* than a booty call, but if it turned into us having sex, all the better for me!"

Figures.

Towards the end of our two-hour conversation, he asked me out. Of course I had seen this coming - using predictability instead of intuition - and I was ready for it.

"Noooope. I don't trust you and I don't wanna open myself up to that kind of pain again. You, my friend, are no longer inside the circle of trust."

I briefly thought about giving him Rya's phone number. If she bought what he was selling, *maybe* I would consider taking a chance. Ultimately, I decided against it because she would have eaten him for dinner before he even knew he was on the menu. Tempting as the thought was, the decision was mine to make.

"Can I call you again?" he asked.

Not so fast, speed racer.

"Did you cheat on me?"

I could almost see him shaking his head when he answered, "Nope. I didn't. I broke up with you before I met with my ex-girlfriend. Even then nothing happened because she didn't want a romantic relationship. In fact, she returned to her ex-boyfriend and they got married."

A Cheshire cat smile bloomed on my face. *Karma's a bitch.*

"Can I call you again?" he repeated.

"Look. The only reason I'm *even* considering this is because you had the decency not to cheat on me."

"So, is that a yes?"

Persistent, aren't you?

Dodging his question, I asked one of my own. "Trinity? It's nice to reconnect. But I feel like you're holding something back. What is it you're not telling me?"

In the past, I might have let this slide, but I wasn't that woman anymore.

On the other end of the line, there was a deep inhalation, followed by a lengthy silence. When he responded, his voice sounded strangled.

"Losing you was the stupidest thing I've ever done, and I deeply regret it."

He had said it earlier, but this time he made sure I knew he meant it.

Satisfied, I now answered his question.

"Yes, you may call me again."

As we said our goodnights, a sense of completion came over me. I had said what I needed to say, and whether he called again or not, it didn't matter, not really, as I had been true to myself and had finally obtained closure. I could now fully move forward without his memory haunting me.

My sleep was spotty, too many unearthed memories, and the next day I turned to my tarot cards for some answers. After shuffling, I drew two random cards: "Romance" and "Happily Ever After." But instead of the wide-eyed excitement I previously felt, I now viewed them with a jaded – and much wiser – eye.

Experience had taught me that when Trinity was involved, things don't often go as predicted.

CHAPTER 21

The following week, after several marathon phone calls where we covered large expanses of emotional ground, I agreed to have supper with Trinity.

The night of our date I took my time getting ready. I carefully applied makeup and styled my hair so it looked as if I hadn't primped. I dressed casually but alluringly in a pair of trendy, low-rise jeans and a baseball-like top that hugged my small curves and slender waist. My only accessory was a can't-be-without tube of lip balm tucked into my front pocket.

I managed to keep my nervous energy under control until I heard the growl of a Harley Davidson motor and looked out my window. Sweet Jesus, he had ridden his motorcycle. Knowing this spelled trouble, I looked to the ceiling in a silent entreaty. Then I watched as he took off his helmet and glanced toward my apartment windows. Fearing he would see me gawking, I hastily stepped back and thought, *Would you look at him? Daaaaamn.* He was even more savagely handsome than I remembered.

I let out a squeal of excitement and began jumping up and down like a human pogo stick. *Geez, when did it get so hot in here?* As the buzzer to my apartment sounded, I stopped bouncing, checked my appearance, and broke into an enormous grin.

This is happening! Oh my God. Thank you, THANK YOU! He's here! He's finally here!!

Not wanting to appear as if I was excited to see him, I did a few high knees to work through the jitters and kept the door closed until he knocked. When he did, I took a deep breath, held it, and then slowly exhaled. I opened the door and instantly felt his magnetism wash over me. My breath caught, my knees weakened, and my heart slammed into my ribcage.

Oh my God.

Despite this, I managed a casual greeting as Trinity breezed across the threshold. Drinking him in, I noticed his square jawline was accentuated by a recent haircut and his bronzed, freckled cheeks enhanced his hazel eyes, which, by the way, were currently giving my face an appreciative look. And finally, I took in his impish, dimpled grin that was both disarming and bewitching.

Mayday, MAYDAY!

"Hi!" he cheerfully replied as he took in my carefully crafted appearance.

Yep, that's right. You gave all of this up. Now you wanna play? Okay. Let's dance.

As we were putting on our helmets it struck me that the motorcycle ride was not merely transportation, it was also calculated foreplay. He wanted my toned legs straddling his thighs and hips. He wanted my B-cups pushing into his back when he playfully tweaked the hand brakes. He wanted my hands around his waist (or chest) when he purposely accelerated too fast, and he wanted my body to mold into his when the night air turned chilly.

The motorcycle ride ended with me at his apartment where Trinity opened a bottle of red wine and set out some artisan cheese and crackers. We sat on the leather couch, knees touching, and taking each other in with our hungry eyes. As we chatted about everyday things, I thought, *Is this really happening?*

The plan was to take it slow and I really tried, but there was no stopping the seduction and truthfully, I didn't want to. Somewhere between bites of cheese and sips of wine, with Grey's Anatomy on the television, his lips found mine, my reserve faltered, and our clothes fell to the floor.

CHAPTER 22

I am a huge Seinfeld fan, and one of my favorite episodes is when George Costanza looks at his life, declares it a disaster, and decides to start doing the exact opposite of what he would normally do. Miraculously, things start to turn around: he gets the usually unobtainable girl and lands a job he's not qualified for. This approach was not so different from what Susie had been teaching me. In a nod to the show, I called it "Doing The George" or, for the few of you not familiar with Seinfeldian antics, "Fake It Until You Make It."

As much as I enjoyed the screenwriter's concept, doing it in real life was a completely different story. I had been born without the patience gene, and though time and Acts of God (literally) had allowed me to improve, it still wasn't easy waiting for results. That said, realizing the benefits of patience, coupled with the fact that I now had someone to practice on, made it more enticing.

I started using The George on Trinity by refusing to call him after our reconciliation sleepover. Deciding my mom's wisdom wasn't so outdated after all, I let him chase me. Then, in another performance of a lifetime, I remained slightly aloof when we were together. After all, we may be seeing each other again, but my heart was still on the shelf.

But, as I said before, old habits die hard. There were many times when I picked up the phone and dialed his number, only to hang up before pressing send. I would then stomp around my apartment, cursing Trinity and crying because I feared he was going to abandon me again. When these thoughts crossed my mind, logic would thankfully intervene and tell me I was being neurotic. *Melissa, when he broke up with you, he told you. Him not calling doesn't mean he doesn't wanna be with you or that he's found someone better. It could mean a multitude of things. Have patience. Trust.*

These frequent self-talks were important and often the reason I kept on Georging. I felt pretty good about all of this until it occurred to me that maybe Trinity *wanted* me to do The George. What if he was thinking, *Awesome! Another girl who likes no-commitment sex. Jackpot!* What if he was beating me at my own game?!

I had over-thought this mess long enough and decided to find clarity by meditating. This alternative stuff was something I scoffed at in my younger years. Surprisingly, as I grew older and more self-controlled, I started to enjoy the quiet my mind achieved and often sought it out for solutions and strength.

At first, I could only meditate for three seconds, which I considered a success, but before long I was up to thirty minutes. By that time, I had let go of censuring and had embraced my curiosity.

Once that occurred, things *really* started to happen. I'd travel to planets that weren't in our solar system and receive insights from powerful Priestesses and sage Elders as well as connected on a deeper level with my angels.

But perhaps the biggest success of meditation was connecting with myself.

That day, as I took some deep breaths, I wondered where my meditation would take me. Sometimes I directed my journeys, but not this time, and within minutes of quieting my mind, I was catapulted to a time when I was five or six years old. I had been experiencing great fear because those that I loved had left me. My mom was often sick and frequently hospitalized, my dad traveled extensively, my brother was in 'Nam, and my sister and grandparents were a state away. Through this meditation, I not only discovered the source of my abandonment issues, but also that, unknowingly, I feared intimacy.

After those amazing revelations, a polished, professional gentleman in a white lab coat appeared. He called himself Dr. Eisenbaum and told me that people came in and out of my life for a reason and a purpose. He said that they were never truly gone, they just existed on a different plane. He reminded me that I am no longer a child, that I can stand strongly and proudly on my own, and that I didn't need anyone to take care of me. After prompting me to affirm that I am strong, powerful, and extremely capable of taking care of myself, he moved on to Trinity.

He deeply loves you, for he has seen your light and he doesn't want to share you with others. He wants to fully commit as he's afraid of losing you. He will be good for you and you should have fun and play. Remember, you are not a child, you can stand alone and are very powerful. You must never forget this.

As the meditation was ending, Dr. Eisenbaum told me to write a book. It would be a cathartic exercise and help me, as well as others, heal a lot of painful memories.

The meditation ended and I felt lighter – and stronger - than I had in a long time. I had made it through the worst, I thought, and was going to write a book about it. But more than that, I was going to help *others* heal, something which thrilled me. Then, with puzzlement, I wondered how those events to date could fill the pages.

Years later, I would question whether Dr. Eisenbaum had only been referring to my past or if he knew about situations that were yet to transpire.

CHAPTER 23

Weeks passed and I was still utilizing The George, but to a lesser degree. Old habits had been replaced by new, more positive ones and things between Trinity and me were going smoothly. Or so I thought. Little did I know that as I evolved, so would The George and I would be using it in a new way.

Without my knowledge, and shortly after another forward-looking conversation about having children together, Trinity scheduled a vasectomy.

As you can imagine, I was devastated by both his decision and his choice to exclude me, especially since I had been abundantly clear that I wanted children, or at least the chance to have them with him, and he had repeatedly assured me he was on board. Obviously, something had changed.

He had, once again, opted to use the phone instead of delivering this unpleasant news face to face. As the sucker punch made contact, blood drained from my face as my hand went to my forehead and began rubbing a small area. Two months had passed since we had reconciled, and, like before, we were making long-term plans, however, his one-sidedness was certainly going to change that.

But, true to form, I didn't yell or argue; I simply mumbled, "Uhhh, ummm, I, I need to go." Then, without waiting for his response, I disconnected and stared blindly at the kitchen counter. My body broke into a cold sweat and my mind repeated one word: *Why?*

After what felt like hours, but was only minutes, the stupor broke and the tears came, bringing with them my old enemy: fear. Having come far in my approach with conflict, I had yet to face something of this magnitude, and I sought to escape the conversation I knew we must have.

I wish I was dead.

I allowed this thought for mere moments before my mind changed direction and focused on my guardian angels. In disbelief, I wondered how they could allow me to get back together with Trinity, only to effectively allow our relationship to end. How was this supposed to work if he kept doing things to break us apart?

Once again, I reached out to Rya and Susie for their opinions. Rya was the realist: "He's going to do what he's going to do and you're going to do what you're going to do because of it."

Susie was the idealist: "Don't give up hope. Nothing is as it seems. It looks like Trinity really doesn't want to have this vasectomy, but he's afraid of how much he feels for you, Missy Pooh. He's also afraid you're not real and that you'll transform into something horrible, as others have done, and he's dealing with that by running away. I'll say it again; all is not as it seems. Try and remain calm, keep doing The George and, when you're ready, talk with him."

They were both correct, but Susie's message confirmed what I had suspected but didn't want to acknowledge: Trinity, after all we had overcome, was pushing me away, again. Immediately my grief turned to anger, and I found myself furious with his level of cowardice.

Meditation was what I needed and, once again, the Guys came through.

We assure you, little one, he does not want this. He will realize your love is infinitely more important to him. You will not fail, little one. You cannot fail. He is open and receptive to you. He is looking for a way out of the operation and has just now realized he is suffocating you and pushing you away. He is horrified at his actions, but he does not know what to do to stop it.

Talk with him from the heart. He will listen, and you will be heard. He has such love for you. We assure you, all is well. Talk with him. He will listen. You will know what to do and say and he will be infinitely grateful. We urge you to show him your love. He will respond in kind.

He aches to tell you, little one. He is so full of love for you. Let him show you how much he loves you. And he will. All is well. Rest easy, little one. Your time for happiness has come. It is here! Rejoice! ALL IS WELL! Infinite love surrounds you for how can it be any other way, dearest one? You have given so much love and now it is returned one hundred-fold. He cannot envision his future without you in it.

Show him your love, little one. Show him all your beauty and light. He loves you so deeply. Love him back. He will not go through with the vasectomy, as it is not right, and he knows that. He is looking for a way out. Give him one.

A few days later, after no contact, he called and invited me over. I accepted, knowing this was my time to shine. I was not going to let him walk away without a fight. That meant I had to say, calmly and with sincerity, what was in my heart. Mentally, I had been preparing for this, even rehearsing what I wanted to say a hundred times over. Begging my angels for help, I asked them to give me the right words as well as the courage to do what I must.

But even that didn't alleviate the dread.

As we sat close together on his couch, Trinity was ever the salesman who prided himself on successful negotiations. And while he said he was open for discussion, he admitted he couldn't see how we were going to resolve this. I was clear that our relationship would end if he had the vasectomy; he was equally as clear that he was going to have the operation. We were at an impasse.

"*I know* we are supposed to have a baby together," I implored, "and I know it'll be a girl."

"I've always wanted a girl."

Drawing fuel from this, I said, "Please, *please* don't do this! It's not right. There have been too many signs indicating this is not right.

Please rethink this. We are destined to have a baby; she's waiting for us. PLEASE DON'T DO THIS!"

My impassioned words had no effect on his decisive mind; the operation would take place as planned. Realizing this was not the time to retreat, I decided to tell him I loved him. Unfortunately, when I did, he thought I was being calculating and viewed the admission as a way of trying to manipulate and control him, as so many others in his life had done.

This couldn't be farther from the truth – I didn't operate that way – but he pulled away all the same. Withdrawing his hand from mine, he moved to the other side of the sofa. I watched as his eyes became shielded and knew he was shutting down. After waiting for what felt like decades to tell him I loved him, I had triggered something deeply painful within him.

And yet, all I could think to do was tell him again. Avoiding eye contact and refusing to touch me, he maintained emotional distance as he murmured, "I care deeply for you."

Upon hearing this, and though I was careful not to show it, my head exploded into a mass of red-hot anger. Telepathically I shouted at him, *Come on, Trinity! Step* UP! *Stop it with this fear-based shit. It doesn't serve you. "You care deeply for me." Bull*shit! *I know you love me, you stubborn ass, so own it! Haven't you learned anything from my struggles? Stop trying to escape and just deal with it!*

I wondered if I had gotten through to him, because he quickly switched from being serious into the much safer role of playful. Though he could no doubt see the steel in my gaze and the hurt on my face, he tried another avoidance tactic; he wanted to make love. I, on the other hand, was too wounded. Wanting to retreat to the safety of my apartment in order to lick my wounds, I placed a gentle kiss on his unyielding lips and whispered, "I love you."

He said nothing.

"Will you call me when the surgery is over? Please?" I asked.

"Yes," he said after hesitating.

"Do you promise?"

He nodded his head and then, twisting the knife, said, "I need a ride to the hospital. Can you do that?"

Are you fuckin' serious?!

"No, I can't. That's asking too much. I'm sorry."

Once home, I crawled into bed where I curled into the fetal position and thought about the words to another Kelly Clarkson hit: *I wanna man who's gonna stand by my side, not a boy who's gonna run and hide.* I was disappointed in my angels, in myself and, most of all, in Trinity. I had come all this way only to let the man I cherished, the man I loved, slip away.

Feeling like a failure, I turned my exasperation heavenward, *What the blue balls FUCK, you Guys?! You said this would go well! You said I wouldn't fail. You promised! What the hell happened?!*

My displeasure spent, I then cried myself to sleep.

As is often the case, all was not as it seemed. My angels may not have foreseen Trinity's duck and cover maneuver, but they were quick to recover and were already working on plan B.

CHAPTER 24

Upon waking, I saw a translucent queen at the foot of my bed. On top of her blonde head was an ornate golden crown and on her back were large, dragonfly-like gossamer wings. Off in the distance, I could see a magnificent horse-drawn carriage. Returning my gaze to her, I noticed her alabaster skin and dazzling smile, but it was her vivid blue eyes that held my attention. In one hand she carried a wand with a shiny, glittering silver star at the tip. She began moving it in slow, small circles and as she did, the star began emitting brilliant silver, gold, green and pink sparks that landed lightly on me, giving me an instantaneous sense of calm and a knowing that, *without a doubt,* Trinity wouldn't go through with the vasectomy.

Having communicated her message, she faded from view and left me staring in silence. The Guys had told me the same thing earlier, along with reassurances that I had done a beautiful job, but I was inconsolable. Not letting that stop them, they continued by saying Trinity struggled with fears of being controlled and detested women who tried to dominate him. Our recent interaction had offered him a chance to change because I had opened a door from which golden light emanated. It was up to him, they said, to choose whether he stepped through, leaving his old life behind. While he decided, I was urged to remain calm and to keep doing The George.

To make sure I knew I wasn't alone and that I was supported, the Guys showed me orange, threes, and repeatedly played the song "You Gotta Be" by Des'ree, all in the span of a few short hours.

A day went by, then two, and still no contact from Trinity. As instructed, I was doing The George but even that was wearing thin. I needed to know what was going on and for that I turned to meditation.

Your One sees the future with you and it's becoming clearer to him. He loves you completely and is scared to tell you. He fears so much. You are here to unlock him and help him. He is already changing, he is facing some of his fears. He cannot imagine a future without you in it. He loves your strength and gentleness. He is coming out of a cocoon, kind of as if he's waking up and really seeing the world around him. He's gaining strength and you are directly responsible for that.

Finding solace in this, I thought, *Where would I be without these intuitive gifts?*

Within a week of our last conversation, Trinity's surgery date arrived. My mood matched the weather: overcast, blustery and raw. Unable to eat, I paced, chewed my fingernails, and worried. Rya checked in with me, as did Susie, but neither of them could lift the oppressive fog.

"Sus?" I asked. "What do you see? Is he gonna go through with it?"

"I'm seeing an operating room but before I can tell if Trinity is there, a white sheet descends, obscuring my view. I can't see beyond it. I'm sorry, sweetie."

As the day stretched into eternity, I found myself staring at the phone. By evening, unable to take another moment of this, I decided to meditate.

Oh, little one! This is truly a joyous moment. He has stepped up into his spiritualness. This is truly a miracle. We see you two getting closer and committing. You will know the truth of what we say soon. You prayed for a miracle and this is it! Rejoice, little one! Rejoice! Truly resplendent!

Unable to help myself, I asked them to prove it.

"Let a red vehicle drive by within the next thirty seconds, please." I then looked out my apartment window and instantly noticed a red pickup parked on the street. *No, that's not it,* I thought as I turned my attention to the busy road and then, as if right on cue, a red sedan drove by.

Thinking this was a fluke, I ordered, "Show me another."

Within moments, not one, but two more red vehicles drove by. *There are my signs! Trinity didn't have a vasectomy!*

Except that he did.

Of course I didn't know this. Filled with joy, I headed for bed and as I did, I passed by the phone and willed it to ring with the promised call. It remained silent. The next morning, I understood why. Trinity had opted to send a short email instead, thereby sidestepping any verbal encounters.

"Everything went well. My back is sore, but I'm at work today."

Well good for you, Mr. Promise Breaker! Mr. Dream Crusher. Mr. Avoider! Good for frickin' *you.*

After reading his words, the elation I previously knew fell flat. I slid from the chair and sank like a lifeless blob to the floor. While there, I felt the sting of what I viewed as another betrayal by the Guys. As tears fell, I begged God to take me Home as this life was turning out to be overly cruel.

After discussing this turn of events with an equally devastated Susie, she asked how often the Guys had been wrong. She knew the answer, of course, but she needed me to acknowledge it.

"Never," I replied.

"The Guys see the entire road map, Missy Pooh, not just a street as we do. Due to this, all may appear to have been lost, but just when you think the road ends, there will be a bridge and it will take you to the other side."

And she, I would later learn, was not wrong.

CHAPTER 25

The first time Trinity had ended our relationship he had done so by using the pretense of another woman. This time, he was using a vasectomy to avoid facing his fears. By continuing to do things the old way, our relationship was an emotional rollercoaster that had me in a complete tizzy.

I saw Trinity as a powerful man, an Alpha. He was my hero, my warrior, my champion. But he saw himself through an outdated lens. He believed he would never be good enough, *loveable* enough, and he continued to struggle against feelings of being controlled and manipulated. He, like many of us, had learned that avoidance was infinitely easier than facing a problem. Unfortunately, that couldn't be further from the truth. If avoidance is chosen, your problems will grow, and so will the strength needed to overcome. On this I speak from a lifetime of experience.

I chose not to respond to his email and, in the days that followed, I operated on autopilot; it was either that or collapse. In meditation I was told, *All is not as it seems. Keep going!* I met that with pursed lips, a raised middle finger, and a bunch of swear words. *Why am I even meditating when it just feels like a sham?*

Wherever I went and whatever I did, I couldn't seem to escape my distressing situation. I went to the gym, where the pitiless televisions played ads for pregnancy tests, diapers and the show

"A Baby Story." Seeking another form of distraction, I picked up a magazine and opened it to a page with an article about raising children.

Oh yeah? Well, fuck you, Guys, I thought as a tear fell. *Fuck you, one and all.*

The truth was, I should have spent less time cursing them and more time listening. They were trying to help by showing me signs that all *was* well. But I was in such a deep state of grief that I couldn't see anything other than what I wanted to see.

I should have known they would *never ever* do anything to hurt me, or anyone else, for that matter.

Having earlier read that only ten percent of men go through with vasectomies, I wondered why Trinity was such a fucking nonconformist. *I hate him,* I thought, I hate him for playing small and weak and for running from issues even after all the talks we had about facing them. I hate him for being so damn selfish and refusing to see how his immature actions hurt me.

Then, with my eyes threatening to overflow, I thought, *I hate him for wrecking my dreams and breaking my forgiving heart . . . again.*

Unable to see the treadmill any longer, my workout ended.

Upon returning to my apartment, I saw my answering machine's light was blinking. I checked caller ID and saw Trinity had called. I stared at the blinking red light for what felt like minutes, weighing whether I wanted to listen. I opted not to because I needed to keep some distance between us. I just couldn't face anything more right now.

Deciding to do a tarot spread, I walked into the office and grabbed my angel cards. That was odd, I thought, because my go-to cards were the fairy ones. They brought sweet, gentle and playful energy. In contrast, the angel cards were more disciplined and serious. As I shuffled,

I internally said, *I'm gonna draw three cards. What do you need me to know*? Their answer was:

"*#1. Assertiveness* - This situation can be healed gently and with love as you've requested, yet there's also a need for your strength and truthfulness with the other person involved. We, the angels, will stand behind you as you speak your truth, giving you strength and guiding your words.

#2 Giving and Receiving - This card is letting you know that giving and receiving are out of balance. There is a situation in your life that requires balance.

#3. Opportunity to Forgive - This situation brings you the opportunity to heal, grow, and release negative patterns. Hold the intention of seeing the other person's inner Divine light and goodness. We (the angels) will help you release unforgiving thoughts, feelings and energies, and lift you to a higher place of peace and compassion.

You are tired of being in a recurring negative pattern in your life. You are asked to let go of the old toxic thoughts about a current relationship or situation. There is no need for blaming you or the other one involved. You are able to release the anger, worry, and fear by breathing it out.

Ask your guides and angels to take it away. When you release it all, there will be a creative solution to this situation. Even though you are asked to forgive this person/situation, in no way does it mean that you're saying what was done was okay. It just means you are no longer willing to carry around all the toxic feelings or thoughts about it. There is a hidden blessing in this relationship/situation."

My shoulders sagged, my head fell backwards, and I slumped forward in my chair. With eyes closed, I inhaled, letting the breath swell my tummy. As I exhaled, I opened my eyes, readjusted my head and straightened my shoulders. These cards were tangible; they were real. I couldn't make up their meaning or make them appear, and I couldn't misinterpret them. Out of forty-four cards, "someone" had chosen the perfect three. Fortunately, even I couldn't dispute that because trusting propelled me forward in ways arguing couldn't.

I rose from my swivel chair, left the office and walked directly to the answering machine where I pressed play only to discover no message had been left; it was just dead air. Instead of feeling sadness, I felt relief. After all, I had stuff to think about, work through and let go. I'd had enough of this day, too, so I headed to bed where I could sleep away the heartache.

Unknowingly, by facing this issue, I was allowing a stronger, courageous and more resilient me to emerge, just as I had that night in the walk-in closet all those years earlier. Those traits would serve me well in the years to come, when Trinity would "encourage" me to grow again.

CHAPTER 26

At 3:33 in the morning, I was roused from sleep by a booming baritone voice. *Expect a miracle for it has been delivered.* I was then shown an image of a beautifully wrapped present on the other side of my apartment door. In shiny, pearl-white opalescent paper, complete with an ornately tied mauve satin ribbon and bow, the gift was the size of a hatbox. Its appearance was so real that I left my bed and opened the door, fully expecting the package to be there. When it wasn't, I looked up and down the hallway, shrugged, shook my head, shut the door and went back to bed.

In the morning, the mysterious "miracle box" was still on my mind. Retracing last night's steps, I opened the door and, again, found nothing there. Not understanding what the vision meant, I trusted it would someday be revealed.

With that, I went into my office to meditate. This time, I was piloting a ship from the 1800s, the kind used by pirates and the English navy. The Guys pointed out the beauty of the ship. *Look at the sleek lines, the well-polished wood, the clean deck and full, well-repaired sails. You built this ship and she is as much a part of you as your own identity. You know her like the back of your hand.*

Your fine ship has a rat problem deep within her bowels. Do you feel this diminishes her beauty? If so, would you wreck it on the shoals or beach it on the sand just to get rid of the rats?

As I was shaking my head, they continued. *Every ship has rat problems, but they keep to the belly of the ship. We will shine our light on them, illuminating them and thereby killing them.* I was then shown the ship's hold, where beacons were shining in every dark, recessed corner. *If you were to wreck this ship, the rats would just swim to the next one. The only way to truly be rid of them is to shine a light on them, see them for what they are, call them out of the darkness, and deal with them.*

Your One is right beside you, for you built this handsome and formidable ship together. It is powered by God's love (it fills the sails) and the hold is full of food (energy). The storm is behind you and there is clear, calm sailing ahead. Continue just as you are; stay up top and steer the ship while we reduce the rat population below.

This meditation did more than just illuminate vermin, it also made two things very clear. First, no relationship is without fear and by facing that, it goes away. If you choose to wreck the relationship without dealing with the "rats," then they would not only survive, but multiply, and eventually overrun the new ship.

Damn, these Guys were good.

And second, I needed to contact Trinity. Not feeling strong enough to do that over the phone, I composed an email telling him that I needed him.

"I'm lost," I wrote, "and I instinctively know you're the only one who can help me. I need your compassion, support, strength and love. But most of all, I need you next to me. I love you, I need you, I want you, I miss you."

Feeling proud of myself for being vulnerable in a time where I didn't want to be, I sent the message and waited for his reply. I was hoping Trinity would feel the genuineness of my words and respond in kind, but his sarcastic, immature and emotionally cold response told me I had expected too much.

As I read his message, I knew it was designed to hurt me, an unconscious reaction to his feeling harmed. Filling with anger, I thought, *Goddammit*! How can he be so *childish*?!

Deep breath . . . deep breath, Melissa.

Clearly the email approach hadn't worked, so I reluctantly picked up the phone.

On the third ring, Mr. Vasectomy answered.

"Hi! How are you?" I said, even though I really didn't care. Without waiting for his response, I asked if we could talk and then said I needed him.

"I don't think we have anything to talk about," he said callously. "You made it very clear where we stood if I had a vasectomy."

Hearing both his tone and his words, I knew our relationship was finished. Intending to say just that, I took in a steadying breath and said, "I'm not ready to make that decision yet. I wanna walk the path with you a little longer. I need to see where we might go before I make that decision. Are you able to walk this path with me for a little while longer, just to see how things go?"

Then, having no conscious thought of forming those words, my breath caught, and my eyes went wide with alarm. *Uhhh, what just happened?* That's *not* what I was gonna say. WHO THE HELL TOOK OVER MY BRAIN?!

Thinking it was somehow the phone's fault, I quickly scrutinized it and deemed it uninhabited by aliens. Still confused, I returned it to my ear and thought that even though the words weren't mine, they felt right.

Possibly feeling the same way, Trinity said, after a lengthy pause, that he'd be willing to do this, but he didn't want to hold me back from having children. And this time, with words I remember forming, I said that I understood and would still like to continue.

With that business out of the way, Trinity invited me over and I jumped at the chance. On the way there, I knew I needed to talk with him about his emailed response, but I also knew I needed his touch.

The moment I saw him, all thoughts of talking went right out the window. For almost two weeks I had believed I was destined to live without him, and now, having been given another chance, his presence was a powerful aphrodisiac. Marching up to him, I grabbed the top of his shirt and pulled his muscular frame towards me, raised my hands to the sides of his face and then crushed his lips to mine. As we kissed passionately, I undressed.

I grabbed his hand and led him into the bedroom where I thought about ripping his shirt's buttons off. Instead, I rapidly began unbuttoning them and continued on with his jeans. Thirsty for him, I didn't want any foreplay, something which Trinity was only too happy to oblige.

Afterwards, as we snuggled, I decided it was time to tackle his email. Taking a deep breath, I said, "I have to talk with you about something. I get that when girls are getting into something emotional, guys wanna run. But here's what I really need the next time I'm vulnerable, or the next time I tell you I need you. I need you to *empathize* with me. I need to feel as if you understand. How about I help you with this the next time it happens? Would that be okay?"

He nodded and with a mischievous grin, began kissing me again. All thoughts of additional conversation were instantly lost.

CHAPTER 27

The days that followed seemed to blend into others, and each one seemed to bring new, positive changes for us as individuals and as a couple. Out of the blue, Trinity would call just to ask how my day was, or to let me know he was thinking of me. I reveled in these and other tender gestures because they showed his unspoken love for me.

I continued to work The George and at some point, it had started weaving itself into my genetic tapestry. For example, when Trinity was unable to keep plans, I'd honestly say, "No problem. Do what ya gotta do," instead of, "What?! Again?!" By doing this I was breaking, and possibly eliminating learned, habitual responses and gaining mental space.

Since art imitates life, it was only a matter of time before I felt the need to declutter my personal space as well.

This happened not long after Rya's daughter had announced that my home, with its Elizabethan décor, looked like an old person lived there. Looking around, I couldn't help but agree and within a month's time I had removed all that no longer felt right. China, crystal, doilies, bedding, vases, silverware, and so on went out the door, eventually replaced by more contemporary items. My personal style was changing as well; gone were the days of mom jeans and high-necked, conservative, and loose-fitting clothes. I also no longer wanted a quilted bedspread, pink bath towels and a bevy of framed photographs. With that completed, I then looked at my diet and decided to consider becoming a vegetarian.

All of this could be credited to my spiritual evolution, Reiki journey, and of course, doing The George.

Just as I'd suspected four years earlier when leaving the doctor's office, Reiki had been the answer to my career prayers and my true calling. During the months Trinity and I were apart, and after overcoming much trepidation, I opened Inner Focus Reiki, where I was continually blessed with clients who affirmed my innate need to combine energy work with intuitive gifts. It was this unwavering desire that allowed me to find my passion and it set me apart from others by allowing me to help in ways they couldn't.

Deciding to become self-employed, something I had never wanted to do, and admitting to others I was an intuitive, was a trust walk. In the beginning, while I was still taking Reiki classes, I would nervously practice on my closest and most trusted friends. With their permission, I would incorporate my intuitive abilities and their feedback was phenomenal: eyes grew wide and mouths dropped. I repeatedly heard, "How'd you *know* that!?" I would shrug my shoulders and truthfully say, "I dunno." Over time, I noticed that the validating intuitive information brought a whole new level to a person's healing. As was the case with me, I discovered when you heal an emotion, the disease often vanishes.

With practice, my confidence grew, and I decided to branch out to family, acquaintances and then to strangers. Interestingly, I found doing intuitive work on them was often easier than on besties. With a stranger, there was no questioning whether I had somehow known the information because of our relationship.

Shortly after the completion of Reiki training and obtaining the Reiki Master designation, Susie, a consummate party-thrower with a love for connecting people, hosted a casual event in her backyard. After giving this a lot of thought, I decided I wanted to try my skills on those who were in attendance. I was hesitant about this as most of those individuals were Susie's clients and I didn't want to appear as if I was trying to take business away from her.

With hands clasped to hide their shaking, I asked Susie if it was acceptable for me to do some readings on her friends. She, ever the supporter, enthusiastically gave me the approval. After selecting three (that freaking number!) random people and after receiving permission, I delivered their angelic messages. All three were amazed and thankful and it was then that I knew I was ready to go public.

Another hurdle was believing my guardian angels would show up, each and every time. This, given my abandonment and betrayal issues, was one of my biggest concerns. The other was telling my conservative dad that I was eschewing Corporate America for a holistic healing business where I would be talking with angels and deceased people.

CHAPTER 28

At Trinity's two-month post-op vasectomy appointment, the test results showed he still had swimmers. "Completely normal," the doctor had assured him. Each time we made love, I would pray, *Please, God. Please. Let me get pregnant before it's too late.* The chances of this were unlikely as we were faithfully using birth control, but I also trusted that if it was meant to be, it would be.

A month later, after another follow-up exam, Trinity and I were having supper. In between bites of food, he ever so casually mentioned that his sperm count was higher than it had been pre-op.

"What does that mean?" I asked.

It was then, after months of wondering, that the contents of the beautifully-wrapped invisible gift box were revealed.

"Ummm. It means the vasectomy didn't work."

I rocketed forward in my seat, eyes wide and face split into an astonished grin.

"*Whaaaaaaat?!*" I sputtered, even though I had clearly heard him.

Without waiting for him to continue, I sat back, folded my arms and with a smug look said, "Told you so. TOLD YOU SO! I *told* you that you weren't supposed to do it! I told you it wasn't right. I *fucking* TOLD YOU!"

"The doctors said this rarely happens."

No shit, Sherlock! If you only knew all that went into making this happen.

"I'm starting to believe in your voodoo," he said, somewhat sheepishly.

You don't say!

With a raised eyebrow, I asked, "Do you know *why* it didn't work?"

"I think I have an idea," he said. "The night of the surgery Ian wanted to sleep with me. He hasn't done that in forever so I told him he could. He was restless and kicked me. I think that ruptured the internal stitches."

My mouth gaped and my eyes drilled into his. My mind was processing this and in the span of two breaths, it all became clear.

"Trinity!" I stammered. "Oh my God! The box . . . the gift box the Guys left outside my door. *This* was what was in it. *This* was the miracle they told me to expect!"

Grabbing his hand, I continued, "Oh. My. GOD! The sheer beauty of it all! The angels designed it so that your own son delivers the kick that makes it possible for us to have a child. Holy shit! What are the odds, Trin? Seriously, what are the odds?"

I paused to marvel at the heavenly countermeasures and when I did, Trinity spoke.

"I'm with you; this can't be a coincidence." He drew in a deep breath and finished his thought. "I guess I knew it was wrong. Right from the start it didn't feel right, and I only went through with it because I felt committed."

How'd that work out for ya?

He continued with another revelation. "Having a little girl is something I've always wanted. I want to braid her hair, take her fishing and have her love the outdoors as much as I do." Then, with a sigh, he added, "I should have known better than to go against my gut feelings again."

Looking away from me, and in a voice barely above a whisper, he said, "I knew about a week before I was to get married that it was wrong. I *knew* I shouldn't go through with it. Something was telling me to back out, but I thought it was just pre-wedding jitters, so I ignored it."

With all those disclosures, I knew I wasn't the only one making changes. Trinity was softening his hardened stances, he was allowing in what was previously shut out, and he was facing some insecurities. He was also, unknowingly, manifesting his daughter.

CHAPTER 29

For all his evolution, though, Trinity still hadn't told me he loved me. I continued telling him every chance I got because, for me, the seal had been broken and there was no stopping the flow. For him, an Eagle Scout who loved fishing, hiking and camping, he needed to see how I performed in the great outdoors before saying those three little words. Hiking I could get behind, but fishing was never my thing and tent camping? Is that when you stay at a Holiday Inn instead of a Radisson Blu?

An inaugural outing was organized. He took it easy on me (or himself) by planning a day excursion where we could utilize his newly purchased canoe. On a cloudy, windy early spring day, we headed to a small North Dakota lake. We packed a lunch, brought sunflower seeds (a staple, I was told), beer and, just in case we underestimated the elements, additional warm clothes.

Not liking the weather or the outing's itinerary, I shut my yapper and kept an open mind, employing a little bit of The George. Trinity wasn't bothered by the conditions, instead he was as giddy as a kid in a candy store: new paddles and extensively researched life jackets awaited, and, of course, determining the boat's seaworthiness. But what he was most excited about, I thought, was to see if I was (another famous Seinfeld reference) "sponge-worthy."

We were thoroughly enjoying ourselves in a way that can only happen in the early stages of a relationship. The small lake's waves were white-capping, and the wind was bone-chilling. Oblivious, Trinity was trying to impress me with his knowledge of paddling, and I was acting like I cared when really I was inwardly wishing for death, his or mine, it didn't matter much if it ended the outing. *Why am I doing this, exactly?* I thought. *Ooooh yeah. Performing some Neanderthal love test.*

About an hour after we began, Trinity set a new course: the shoreline reeds. Coaching the canoe from the middle of the lake, I hoped their density would provide a modicum of shelter. Instead, they became our Waterloo.

"Fish love to hang out in the reeds," he said as he was reaching for a handful of them. Intending to pull us deeper into the natural cover, he instead capsized the canoe.

With panic on our faces, we quickly realized we were in relatively shallow water and easily found our footing. Standing, we watched our lunch and sunflower seeds float away, and then began laughing at the silliness of the situation. The laughter faded along with our warmth: the water was barely above freezing, we were drenched and shivering from head to toe. And even though my fingernails were turning blue, I didn't say a single negative word (out loud, that is). However, if I hadn't actively been practicing The George, his head would have been floating right along with our food.

After hauling the canoe to shore, Trinity suggested that I sit in the warmth of the car and he didn't have to ask twice. As I changed out of my clinging and sodden clothing, I thought, *Who the hell am I?* Then, trying to be optimistic, *Ooooh, this is an adventure. I'm with my man!* But my mind pushed back, momentarily abandoning The George, and as Trinity was putting the boat on the roof rack, I snarled through clenched teeth, "I fuckin' *hate* shit like this!"

Hearing none of that, Trinity entered the car in great spirits, but I noticed when he changed his clothes, his hands were trembling and that he kept fumbling with the heating controls, as if he thought they were broken. Our drive home was filled with unnatural quiet, each lost in our own thoughts. Once back at his apartment, we took a hot shower (together, of course!), and since neither of us was feeling the best, we brushed our teeth, snuggled into his comfortable queen-sized bed and fell asleep.

Not much later I was awoken by cramping intestines. Feeling as if they may give birth, I thought, *What the hell?* Glancing at Trinity, I saw that he was sleeping peacefully. *Thank you, baby Jesus, for that small kindness.* Another stroke of luck was that Trinity's apartment had two bathrooms. That meant I could spare myself the indignity of having him wake to the enjoyable sounds of diarrhea.

Sprinting to the furthest bathroom, I took care of the working end of things.

Well, this is lovely. I must have swallowed some lake water and now I have the shits.

When I was relatively sure I could make it back to bed, I resituated my clothes, washed my hands and walked to the bedroom. Noticing Trinity was still sleeping, I crawled in and reclaimed my position, then, closing my eyes, I let out a sigh of relief just before another cramp ripped across my lower abdomen.

Now thoroughly annoyed, I ripped the covers off, cursing under my breath and exited the bed. *Here we go again! Same song, second verse.* With sphincter puckered, I made a dash for the main bathroom and had the thought that it was much too early in our relationship for Trinity to know I pooped. When I returned, much to my dismay, he was awake.

He sleepily asked, "Are you okay?"

This was embarrassing.

"Um, no."

"What's wrong?"

My face reddened, and I inwardly sighed. "Oh, you know, I . . . um, I seem to have explosive diarrhea."

The bloom was off the rose.

CHAPTER 30

A couple of weeks later, I still wasn't sure whether I'd made it past the qualifying round. That's when Trinity asked if I'd like to go weekend camping and fishing at a Minnesota state park. Apparently not only had I won the bout but was also headed toward the eliminations.

Admittedly, I was a city girl, but I was not the delicate flower I sometimes liked to portray. After all, I had dated several ranchers and farmers and had often milked and branded cows, shoveled manure, herded cattle, tossed hay bales and fried bull's balls. If I could do that, then I could get through two days of camping. Right?

Fishing, though, had never been my thing. My parents, especially my mom, had loved to fish so I grew up with it, but I found it not only exhaustively boring but disgusting as well. I would refuse to touch the bait, and when some poor schmo of a fish took my hook, I would be careful to keep its wiggly, stinky fishiness away from me. With disdain, I would swing the pole toward either parent, then turn my head away as the offending thing was removed.

What I hated the most was their smell. Even the most diluted of fish smells would cause my gag reflex to kick in. I didn't like eating fish either, or their relatives - crabs, oysters, lobsters, prawns, tuna, et cetera. As far as I'm concerned, if it lives in water, it's safe from slaughter.

My parents used to "encourage" me to eat fish or seafood even into my late teens. Posing an exceptional culinary and odiferous struggle was the Christmas holiday, as oyster stew, clam chowder, lobster and lutefisk were the rotating entrees.

Throughout the years, my intense dislike of fish and seafood often earned me incredulous looks. I'd hear horrified gasps of, "Are you insane? How can *anyone* not like seafood?!" I eventually found it was easier to tell people I was allergic; then they'd give me a sad "sucks to be you" smile and drop the subject.

With certainty, fishing held no allure for me. Now Trinity, the love of my life, wanted to test my mettle and see if I'm "I love you" worthy. Okay then, George Costanza it is!

"Trinity, fishing isn't my deal, but because I *love* you, I will make an attempt. However, I'm bringing a book along as backup."

"Deal!"

After Trinity had reserved a campsite for us, we planned our menu and he assigned preparation duties, most of which I was clueless about. I was, however, able to handle the task of making ice cubes. My apartment's fridge didn't have an automatic maker, so I used the plastic trays and made hundreds of them. By golly, you leave this to a Type-A Virgo, and you'll have ice, ice, baby!

I wasn't totally clueless about the camping aspect either. As a child, my parents and I often went to my grandma's somewhat rustic lake cabin where I loved the feeling of freedom and uninhibitedness. The one dedicated chore I had was to mow the lawn, and this was no easy task. The house was located on top of a gentle hill and the little-used boat garage below attracted scads of Martens which dive bombed my thick, chia-pet permed hair if I dared get too close. After my job was complete, though, I was able to do as I wanted and that usually included picking (and eating) raspberries, daydreaming in a hammock and floating on an inner tube.

It was those memories that accompanied me when Trinity and I arrived at our campsite. Amazingly, and maybe partially based on those earlier remembrances, I was in love with everything about it: the trees, the gravel road, the beauty, the coziness and comfortability of it all.

Not knowing exactly what was expected of me, I set up the folding chairs while Trinity set up the tent. I then placed our purchased firewood in the firepit and after a few attempts, started the fire. Proud of myself and thankful for my Girl Scout training, I made myself even more useful by refilling my adult beverage and getting Trinity another beer. It was then I realized I had committed a rookie mistake; camping was all about ease, such as opening an ice-cold beer, not mixing drinks. Despite that, we had our home away from (all the creature comforts of) home set up in no time.

After admiring our handiwork and sipping our beverages, we set off to explore the trails that wound themselves through the park. When we returned, it was time for supper, but I found I was hungry for something else and I didn't have to convince Trinity that food could wait.

Trinity still hadn't told me he loved me, and I juvenilely delighted in telling him that I did. Singing, "I love you, I love you, I loooohuuuuuve you!" like the movie character Elf, I would also leave Lionel Richie-like voicemails telling him, "I just called . . . to say . . . I love you." Emails were signed, "All my love," and yet nothing . . . the big old goose egg in the return department. But this weekend was different; I was positive he would change that.

It had been almost four months since I had told Trinity I loved him. Four *freaking* months! Talk about making a gal work for it! Susie and I had been discussing this, and she felt Trinity was afraid of saying those words because, in the past, people left him or withheld their love. She said he loved me and was committed but saying it out loud made it real, and that scared him.

Seeing the truth in her words caused my heart to sink because I understood this was another battle he was going to have to face or flee. The last woman he had said those words to he married . . . and divorced, a hellish and hostile matter that dragged on for over two years and eventually bankrupted him financially and emotionally.

After that his ex-wife had retreated behind a mask of outrage and hatred and unfortunately, I was often an unwilling witness to

115

her scathing emotional and verbal attacks. The viciousness of these assaults caused me to wonder how she could have once deeply loved, married, and had a child with this man. So yes, if Trinity were to say those words again, he would need to eliminate all thoughts that I would become like her.

Our weekend was amazing; we hiked, canoed, napped, fished (I read a book!), and ate like kings. But still no "I love you." Plans were made to try this camping thing again and I was glad they were. I was really into it and particularly liked who I was away from home. Oddly, I found I liked not brushing my teeth or showering and I discovered using a porta-potty or going potty in the woods wasn't all that bad. In fact, I had even developed a rhythmic way of swishing the toilet paper in order to avoid losing chunks of my hiney to the voracious horse flies. Nothing to it.

About three weeks after our weekend excursion, we decided it was time to try it again. We were able to get the same campsite and were eager for another weekend of rest, relaxation and romance.

After situating ourselves, feasting and stargazing, we called it a day and settled into our two-person tent. The PVC air mattress was creaky and groaned with our every move. Our pillows and sheets wouldn't stay in place, and our fellow campers were noisy, but we loved it all.

As was our way before sleep, we talked for a bit, letting the conversation naturally fade to a comfortable silence. When it did, we kissed goodnight, but this time, instead of turning away after telling Trinity that I loved him, I kept my eyes locked on his.

Now or never, Trinity. Shit or get off the pot. Say the damn words.

I could tell he was wrestling with a big old matzo ball of fear. *Do I tell her and then have her leave me, or worse, turn into a monster and stay? Can I trust that she's different?*

With the decision made, he drew in a breath. "I love you too."

Hallelujah! Finally! Now, where's a phone? I gotta call Rya!

CHAPTER 31

During the months that followed Trinity's admission, life flowed easily. Trinity was continuing to learn and utilize different ways of reacting to issues and stressors. I had taught him to do The George and it was working well for him. He also learned to apply the 24-Hour Rule to things that unsettled or enraged him; consequently, he was becoming less explosive and more tolerant.

After watching *Earthlings*, a movie Rya had recommended, Trinity and I adopted a vegetarian diet. The film showed graphic images of stock animals being grossly maltreated. It also showed how we, in our gluttony, would then waste their meat. Shocked and repulsed, neither one of us could support or be a part of that industry any longer.

Because communication had not been a strong suit in either of our starter marriages (although, at the time, we both thought it was), we agreed to make open and honest conversations, those that would make serving our highest good a priority. We wanted to face everything – good and bad - together and deal with it head-on in the hopes that our relationship would become, as the Guys had said, a "sturdy, well-constructed ship."

A few weeks later, we would be given an opportunity to test that. Trinity, armed with a new meatless recipe, decided to show off his cooking skills. While he was prepping supper, I asked if it would be alright if I transferred pictures from his computer to mine. Approval received, I opened the pictures folder and scanned the contents. I was looking for our latest camping photos but, instead, found images of two people having sex; one of whom was Trinity.

I sucked in a breath as my disbelieving eyes filled with tears. *Oh, sweet Mary, Mother of Christ. I shouldn't be seeing this.* I averted my eyes, but the damage was done.

Looking at Trinity's back, I applied The George. "Umm. I'm not sure what I'm seeing here. Can you help me, please?"

Without hesitation, he turned and walked to me. He glanced at the pictures, smiled and said, "Oh. That's Miss Mankato. We broke up and then got back together."

From the look of things, studly, you sure did!

Returning to his task, he missed the gathering tears in my wounded eyes.

They spilled over and as I began wiping them away, I thought that this must not be a big deal to him. Obviously, I felt differently and with good reason. When Trinity referred to her by an alias he and I had created, I knew she wasn't someone he casually dated; this woman had held a place in his heart. She was also the reason Trinity had delayed his return to me.

Because of that, I couldn't understand why he still had those pictures . . . her pictures . . . *their* pictures when we were in a committed relationship. Thoughts of betrayal and feelings of insecurity were triggered. Did he look at them, I wondered, and did he miss her? Did he trace her face with his finger as I had done to his newspaper photo? But most importantly, was he going to leave me, us, for what they'd had?

Once bitten, twice shy.

He must have sensed something was wrong because the sound of the knife's steady chopping stopped. Returning to me, he noticed the tears and said, "They're just pictures, Melissa. I like to take and keep pictures, that's all."

"This is your deal," I said, "however, when the pictures involve a very private act between a man and a woman and *that* man is the one

I love, I don't want to see them. It bugs me that you're still looking at them. I feel violated."

"I don't look at 'em. Not anymore. I told you, they're just pictures."

"I don't understand why you still have them."

He told me he'd keep all our pictures if something were to happen to us.

Well, isn't that comforting! Thank God there aren't any of us making love and now I know there never will be!

In a daze, I rose from the desk chair, walked to the couch and sank into the coolness of it. What I *really* wanted to do was run as fast as I could. Instead, I applied The George and compromised. I took the recycling outside and then sat in my car where I cried for a few minutes. Feeling somewhat soothed, I wiped my eyes, sulked back into the apartment, avoided eye contact and, once again, fell into the couch.

Again, Trinity stopped what he was doing and sat beside me. In a bit of a snotty tone, he asked, "Why aren't you over this yet?!" When I didn't answer, he left my side and sat in a chair across the room.

His physical and emotional withdrawal loosened my tongue. "I'm allowed to feel how I do. These are my feelings, not yours." And in direct reference to him changing seats, I said, "I shouldn't be made to feel badly about them, either. I love you and I'm deeply hurt that you still have those pictures. I can't give you what you need right now, but I still want you to sit next to me and to touch me."

He moved back to the couch and rested his hand on my knee. He kept repeating, "They're just pictures. They don't mean anything. I don't look at 'em."

Was he telling the truth?

I stared at the carpeted floor, hearing him but not responding. He stood up and walked to his computer. When he came back, he barked, "There! They're gone! When are you gonna snap out of it!?"

I slowly shook my head and through fresh tears replied, "I don't know. I just feel betrayed."

Suddenly, I'd had enough of The George and stood up. I needed some space to figure out why I was having such a huge negative reaction. Kissing his lips, I murmured, "I love you."

He was like granite. He did not return my kiss or words.

I walked to the door thinking, *Oh,* SUPER! *Just great. Perfect time for you to fall back into your old ways and withhold your love. Juuuuuuust fuckin' perfect.*

Within the safety of my apartment, I tried to meditate but each time I closed my eyes, the hurtful X-rated images would cut through the darkness. Becoming frustrated, I turned to the Guys and pleaded, "Help me. Please." Anticipating the worst, I closed my eyes again and discovered nothing awaited. Instead, it was their gentle, combined voice that greeted me.

Calm down, little one. This is just an energy cyst and it will pass. Do not fear or worry over this. It is all good. It is all well. Just a minor blip in your life. Your One does not know how to deal with you when you are sad. He feels frustration that he cannot help you feel better. He does not understand the complexities of you. He feels out of control and lost. He is struggling to find his footing. All is well, you will see. All is exactly as it should be.

Do not fear, do not worry as that will be a major waste of your precious time. You are so loved. Your One loves you so much. He is hurt that he has displeased you. He loves you so. Go to sleep now and do not worry for all is well. All will be revealed by morning light. Dream peacefully for you are truly a Goddess in your Kingdom right now. You rule the roost, so to speak. You are powerful and omnipotent.

This will pass and you two will become as one, stronger and able to bend more easily. Demonstrating their point, I was shown a tall, beautiful tree bending in the wind. *No, little one. Your One will not leave you. Not now. Not ever. He simply cannot exist without you. You are his light and his salvation. All is well.*

A rush of breath escaped me, and I felt calmness returning. My head rolled forward and then circled around my shoulders. Although

I had made great strides trusting the intuitive information, I wanted validation and for that I turned to Susie and Rya.

Susie said Trinity was telling the truth; he hadn't looked at the pictures since I came back into his life. She could understand why he was acting as if they were no big deal and why I was hyperventilating, because guys are so different than girls. Regarding him not returning my kiss, she said it looked like he was trying to figure out how to be with me and it didn't feel right to return my "I love you" or kiss me because he felt that would be pretending everything was fine. Rya echoed this by using a comparison: if Trinity found computer images of me and an ex-lover, he'd be begging me to try some of the positions. Laughing at her truth, I thought, Oh my gosh. Totally!

Sitting with their input, I decided feeling jealous and threatened meant I had something to heal and I needed to deal with those feelings because they had no room in our relationship.

I needed to visit with Trinity about this and that meant a possible confrontation, which scared me tremendously. Talking it through, however, was the only way for me to heal and move forward. Fortunately, Trinity made these things easy for me. Hours after leaving his place, he called and without hesitation, I answered.

"Are you gonna break up with me?" he joked.

"No, silly! I love you." Then, repeating a portion of the Guys' dialogue, I continued, "This was just a little blip in the grand scheme of things. Seeing those pictures, well, I thought you might dump me for her. Evidently, I haven't put all of that behind me yet."

"I love you and I'm never going to leave you," he said with sincerity.

And while I believed him, neither of us were fully aware of how many times he would try.

CHAPTER 32

Another round of spiritual decluttering allowed me to get rid of anger, resentment and other toxic emotions towards Ben. It was then I realized that the death of our marriage wasn't solely on his shoulders; I was equally to blame. A bitter pill to swallow, for sure, but with it came forgiveness, and then, after a period of time, solace.

Somewhere along the way, I had learned that everyone in our life, from the casual acquaintances to major players, all had a role to play. Their purpose might be to help us learn spiritual lessons or to encourage us to become the person we were meant to be. And sometimes, as was the case with Ben, they may push you out of your comfort zone in ways that are truly invidious.

But for all their nastiness on earth, they are our biggest spiritual cheerleaders. They know what we'd like to overcome because, before we were even a twinkle in our parents' eye, a pact was formed and agreed upon by all parties. They were to fight tooth and nail for our success and that meant doing whatever it took to inspire change, for if they failed, and we didn't overcome the issue, then we would repeat these problems, times ten, in another lifetime.

As you can expect, knowing our spiritual life was on the line, and loving us unconditionally, they were vested in honoring their agreement.

With that understanding, came another. Holding on to blame, rage, hatred, jealousy and other low vibratory emotions can cause the youthful to become old, the healthy to become ill, and one's longevity to become diminished.

This process was slow, and only began when I was ready, but once accomplished, I no longer looked at people in my life the same way. Instead, I began seeing what they were trying to help me overcome.

One lazy Sunday afternoon, I shared my newfound wisdom with Trinity during a conversation about our former spouses. I was completely honest, saying I still loved my ex-husband but was no longer *in* love with him. I no longer held any animosity for him either. Instead, I was very appreciative of the role Ben had played in my growth; after all, if he hadn't performed so admirably, I might have stayed.

"I'd like to apologize to Ben for being such a shrew," I said, "and let him know I have deep regrets about how I treated him."

Hearing something other than what was said, Trinity became defensive. "What guarantee do I have that you won't go back to him?"

"That will never happen," I said, knowing his question was prompted by insecurities. "I'm incredibly loyal and, besides, the love I have with you far surpasses what I shared with Ben."

With a nod, Trinity dismissed this topic and brought up my discovery of his sex-with-an-ex pictures. He confessed that my reaction had been a wakeup call, of sorts, inspiring a full-fledged purging spree. He had gone through his computer, closets, drawers and got rid of everything that no longer resonated with him. From there he moved on to his garage, storage locker and even his emotionally exhausting army memorabilia. He admitted that he felt badly about the pain those pictures caused me and wanted to get rid of anything else that might do so.

This made my heart smile. Not only was he looking out for me, he was also following in my footsteps. Booyah, soldier!

Later that day, Trinity announced, "I am incredibly happy. I'm happier than I've been in a long, long time. I'm completely myself around you."

"Humm," I replied teasingly. "Happier than you've *ever* been?!"

"Yeah! Happier than I've ever been. I told you that I loved you and that took me a long time to do."

Really? I hadn't noticed.

"I know you felt it for a long time."

"Yeah, but I didn't *say* it. I've said it now, and I say it often, so that should tell you something. It means I'm not just gonna walk away that easily."

"Will it help you to know that I'm never gonna leave you?" I asked.

He nodded, his beautiful eyes glued to mine.

"Then I need to hear this from you, too," I said. "Given my abandonment issues, it's very important for me to know you'll not leave me. We need to make our relationship a safe, committed place to gr-"

Before I could finish, his phone rang, interrupting our conversation and our connection. My request went unanswered, something that would haunt me in years to come.

CHAPTER 33

. . . Our little light giver. What power you have. What beauty you possess. Have you not grown? Have you not ascended? We tell you that you are truly amazing, and we love that you are spreading your wings and trying to fly. You will grow into them with grace and ease. How could it be any other way? Have you not decreed it? We tell you that you have!"

. . . Abundance is yours and comes to you easily now. Have you not noticed the slight shift? We think you have as you have given thanks to it and for it. Your appreciation is much adored, little one. YOU are much adored. Great whispers of your prowess and greatness are echoing across the land. Take heed! You will be much sought after. Your gifts and your unique way of presenting them will earn you a loyal following. How can it be any other way? You are destined for this and you are destined for greatness.

. . . You were born with the gift that others seek. You have a natural affinity. Do you not already get glimpses of this gift? We think you do as you are starting to yearn for it. That is when you know it is time to seek.

. . . We see your beautiful white wings spreading and flapping. Marvel at your growth for it is truly something to behold. You are doing all the right things, little one, and we assure you, they will come.

. . . You are perfect. We are so proud of you. Take a moment to look at how far you have come. Do you not see the Woman of Strength you

have become? Do you not see how others already seek you and your counsel? They seek you because they trust you and trust is a very, very good thing. You have a special combination of talent that others do not possess. You are so beautiful to us.

. . . You were born to do this. Literally, born to do this. You are so amazing at how you combine all your talents into the persona called you. Is it no wonder people find you? With your amazing grace, charm and gifts of the intuitive nature, you combine all so beautifully and gently. You will be famous, little one.

. . . You have stepped into the stream of abundance. Look around you. Stuff (beauty) just seems to happen. You think about it and it manifests. Do not discount this talent for it is a great gift. You will also help serve mankind with this gift. To get to this point was not an easy task. We ask you, would you have done it differently? We do not think so for look at the beauty that is you right now. Look at how magnificent you have become. The Heavens herald you. You are widely known up here, and word is fast spreading about you on planet Earth. Do not fear. You are ready. You were born ready.

. . . Stay the course, lightworker. Stay the course. It is almost here. Do you feel it? It is upon your doorstep. You were MEANT to do this. Look how beautifully you've grown."

. . . You ask about your Other. He is a constant in your life. He has such deep admiration and respect for you. You are truly his lifeline. You help him and center him when he needs it the most. Before he felt as if he was spiraling out of control. You have shown him another option, another way, and he is most appreciative.

. . . TRUST. There is to be a baby and as you wish, it will be consensual. In fact, he is harboring the secret right now. Give him time to illuminate this secret wish of his. Give him time and watch him grow. You two are destined. Watch for your perfect union to physically materialize soon. He wants you at his side.

. . . He and you will have children. All children are special, but your firstborn (yours and his) will carry on your legacy. It is written

that you will conceive a child at age forty-four. Do not fear. It has no place in your world anymore, for you see, little one, where you are the word "fear" isn't even in the vocabulary. We smile in anticipation of the beautiful miracles you will help to create. You are pure, golden magic. We love you so much.

. . . Our dearest little one. Draw strength from us. We tell you that the gift of life will be yours should you choose. She waits for you even now. She sees the struggles both you and your Other are going through. She knows the inner turmoil both of you have. She understands but she wants you to know that this is destined to happen, and all will be received with love.

. . . Your Other doubts that he will have a healthy child and he will accept nothing less. He knows this is your desire and he is beating himself up because he cannot give this to you. We tell him that yes, he can, and he will give this to you.

. . . There is no greater show of affection than creating another human to carry your legacy. He sees the love in your eyes and knows how much you wish to carry his seed to fruition. Believe it or not, this is the driving force behind many of his decisions of late. He is preparing himself. He will love this baby more than he loves himself.

. . . He loves you so much, little one. He is constantly amazed by you and at the depth of his love for you. You two are a magnificent pair and together will change the world for the better. We are so proud.

CHAPTER 34

My dad was born into a hardworking Norwegian farm family. My mom was also from a diligent farming family, mostly German but part mutt, who lived just miles from my dad.

Dad joined the Army and was sent overseas during WWII. Prior to his deployment, he held a respectable job working for the railroad. He used to frequent a diner where my mom worked and, as the saying goes, swept her off her feet (though she said she only went out with him because she liked his car).

They tied the knot while my dad was on leave. Shortly after that, he returned overseas to continue doing his part for the war effort.

General Patton once asked him if he needed anything. Dad saluted and said, "No sir. Well, maybe some cigarettes, sir."

Without hesitation, Patton turned to his aide and barked out the order.

Once Dad's tour of duty was complete, he returned to his bride and they started a family. Dad resumed his position with the railroad and rapidly received several promotions. Due to that, he often needed to relocate his wife and children to various small towns. By the time I came into the world, Mom and Dad had settled in Williston and my two older siblings were near or at the age of adulthood. My sister married shortly after high school and my brother left for 'Nam. By the time I was three, Mom, Dad and I pulled up stakes as well. Dad had received yet another promotion and we set off for the Twin Cities.

As I mentioned earlier, Mom was not always a healthy woman. She had high blood pressure, angina ("Melissa? Bring me my pills will you, hon?"), bouts of depression and issues with alcohol. Moving a state away was tough on all of us. We lost our physical support system; Mom and Dad left their parents and a daughter behind. I lost my built-in babysitters and playmates, all of which may have played a part in my dance with abandonment.

In trying to cope with my new life, I found an imaginary friend. I don't remember much about this friend, not even whether it was a him or her, but I appreciated the company. When I told adults about what my friend was doing, I'd hear, "What an active imagination you have, Melissa." Not understanding why they couldn't see my playmate, I often insisted what I saw was real. That would be met with a stern "That's enough, Melissa." After several of my parent's admonishments, I thought I must have done something wrong and that, from my experience, often meant punishment. In order to avoid that, I shut out my ethereal friend.

Closing that door opened another, however. When I was in fourth grade, we were learning about the States. One of my classmates, Joe, was a bit of a troublemaker. He would frequently spout off about whatever was on his mind, and had a hard time staying on task or even sitting in his seat. He had just interrupted the class for the umpteenth time when I intuitively knew the unflappable teacher had reached her limit, just as I and the rest of the class had.

I looked at the teacher and knew she was going to give him a hard state to spell. Sure enough, she said, "Joe, please spell Arkansas."

I sensed he couldn't spell it. I watched as he repeatedly stood and sat, and then wrung his fingers. His eyes nervously darted around the room and his tongue flicked out to wet his lips. As we waited for him to answer, I felt the class' exasperation grow. He made a halted attempt and some of our classmates snickered as he failed. He tried again and then once more. I empathically felt his embarrassment and uncomfortableness. *He feels stupid*, I thought, and I felt badly for him.

And, despite my earlier disgust, as he slunk into his chair, I felt an adult-sized flash of anger towards the teacher.

I didn't know this on a conscious level at the time, but my mom was an amazing intuitive. I also didn't know I had more than likely inherited these gifts from her because they are passed down from parent to child. When I was born, I am told, she saw the spark in my eyes and knew I would rise into my power. That knowledge brought her comfort as she had made the decision, long ago, to never use intuitive gifts because she worried that she wouldn't be strong enough to overcome ostracization. Her decision to opt out came at a high price, though. It meant she could not spiritually teach or help me with my inherent gifts. It was a vow she never broke, not even a teensy bit, until prior to her surgery, when she intuitively communicated her earthly departure from the passenger seat of their Caddy.

As a child, I would make clandestine calls to my sister while laying on my mom's side of my parents' double bed. I would dial the memorized number, and with the phone pressed tightly to my ear, I would pray for her to answer. When she did, I would cry and plead with her to come and stay with us. I would tell her I was frightened and that I thought Mom was going to die. My much older sister would do her best to calm me but what she couldn't know, and what I never said, was I constantly worried, as I stated earlier, about who would take care of me if the worst happened.

My sister and maternal grandmother made trips to visit us as often as they could. Sometimes they stayed for days and sometimes for weeks. I felt a sense of normalcy when they were there; I felt protected and safe. As they inevitably prepared to return to their homes, my fears would kick into high gear again.

Also, as a child, I didn't have much of a relationship with my dad. He was gone a lot, and when he was home, he served as the enforcer of physical punishments Mom deemed necessary ("You wait until your dad gets home!"). It's no wonder he both intimidated and mystified me; I didn't even know who he was.

Yet there were incredibly moving moments as well, moments I won't likely forget. Sometimes I would surreptitiously watch him tinker in the garage and listen to his absentminded whistle. Sometimes I would summon the courage to ask if I could help him trim a tree or paint the house. Sometimes I sat on the toilet lid, enraptured by his shaving ritual. And sometimes, when he would pull me onto his lap, snuggle my small frame into his side and then loosely wrap his arms around me, I felt like I was his whole world.

Once, after I had forgotten to put my banana-seated bike with the new flower basket away, he went in search of it while I cried. He found its skeleton behind our backyard hedges. He looked at me, picked up the bike's carcass in one of his big, strong hands (not so big, really, but to a child they were) and walked towards me. Noticing it had been stripped of almost everything, including my cherished white wicker basket, I went from crying to full-on hysterics. He tapped my blond head with two fingers and pragmatically said he'd see what he could do to fix it up again, complete with a new basket. Upon hearing that, my tears slowed, and my heart swelled with gratitude and love.

Another time, around age eight, I became inexplicably lost in a neighborhood that was close to our home yet unfamiliar. A compassionate stranger, who would later become my Girl Scout leader, took me in, wiped my tears and helped dial my family's phone number. After hot chocolate, more tears and some curiosity questions posed to my new friend, I saw our car pull into her driveway and was surprised to see, not my mother's face, but my father's behind the steering wheel. Even more surprising was his relieved expression when he saw me through the picture window, rather than the gritted-teeth anger I had come to expect from him.

Still, I braced myself as he exited the car. Dad was the Punisher, not the Nurturer, and I wasn't eager to hear his harsh words or receive a cuff to the back of my head. I left the house and stood on the steps as he walked towards me with long strides. When he reached me, he bent down and opened his arms. Bursting into fresh tears, I catapulted my pint-sized quivering body into them and then clung to his neck for dear life. Never was I so happy to see my dad, especially since it didn't appear that I was to be reprimanded.

"Are you okay?" he asked.

Keeping my head buried in his neck, I sniffled and nodded, indicating that I was. Returning to the stoic, respectful and mannerly Dad I knew, he uncoiled my arms, stood and extended his right hand to the lady who had helped me. Then he looked down at me and commanded, not unkindly, "Get in the car, Melissa."

I immediately obeyed.

CHAPTER 35

As was the case with many families, my personality was vastly different from my two siblings, as was my "language." Similarly, even at an early age, it was clear to me that Dad and I were speaking in different tongues and neither of us knew how to translate. Although we were not consciously aware of this barrier, Mom was and became a willing interpreter. And while that worked well for everyday stuff, we knew very little of significance about each other. Though I had always loved my dad, our relationship did not begin, in earnest, until the death of my mom.

Our first few phone conversations were jilted and sterile:

"Hi. How are you?"

"I'm fine, how are you?"

"I'm good. What's new?"

"Nothing. What's new with you?"

"Ummm . . . nothing."

You get my drift.

After a few months of communicating this way, Dad and I realized we needed to become fluent in each other's language if we wanted any kind of relationship. Neither of us was aware of this, of course, but the changes began easily; I shared my feelings with him and then he, surprisingly, reciprocated.

When I managed to override my dread and tell him I wanted to open an Intuitive Reiki business where I would work with energy, he amazed me by saying, "Well, can you make money doing that?"

"Yes, Dad. I believe so."

"Well then, good for you!"

Physical touch is my second love language and I've always adored holding hands, giving and receiving hugs, and sitting thigh to thigh. All things Dad wasn't so big on. Throughout the years, I'd watch as he stood back, distancing himself, while Mom and others kept my "hug tank" full. After she died and as Dad's and my translation skills improved, I realized I needed *his* hugs.

I soon found that I was trying to rectify this situation when, on trips home, I would shoulder-bump him. This turned into an awkward shoulder-bump-hand-grab thingy. Then it progressed to resting my forehead on his upper chest for the briefest of moments. As our comfortability grew, the shoulder-bump evolved into a loose translation of a hug. Throughout these progressions, Dad's arms would hang limply.

One afternoon, as I was packing and getting ready to return to Fargo, I felt emboldened to give the Old Man (my pet name for him) a real meat-and-potatoes kind of hug. I threw my arms around his waist and pushed my head into his chest. When his arms remained at his sides, I released mine, reached for his and gently put them around my waist. Then, I repeated the previous scenario but this time, I squeezed tightly. I felt his arms lightly contract around me, just as they had all those years ago when I got lost.

One time, while hugging, I took another bold emotional step by saying, "I love you, Dad."

Never one to say those words, he replied, "Oooh, go on. Get going."

I could hear the grin in his voice, but I wasn't willing to leave it at that. I pulled back and looked up at him.

"Dad. I need to hear it."

"But you know that I love you."

"I know that your actions speak it, yes, but I *need* to hear it."

"Awwwwww . . . go on," he said, clearly uncomfortable.

I released my grip and backed up, careful to maintain eye contact. A smile played about my mouth as my voice took on my mom's warning tone.

"DaaaaaAAAAD!"

He replied in (what I hoped was) fake surrender. "Ooooooh, okay. I love you, too."

Another opportunity to heal an old caustic wound presented itself when my dad, heavily into his cups, misheard something I'd said and let me have it with both barrels.

Eyes welling, I wiped my mouth with my napkin, glanced at my family, excused myself from the supper table and speed-walked to the downstairs guest bedroom. Once there, I let the hot tears flow as I struggled to understand why my dad still had the ability to do that to me. During my childhood, all he had to do was give a certain glance in my direction and my lower lip would quiver. If he narrowed his eyes and added a reprimanding bark, the waterworks started. Now I was in my forties and nothing had changed. Why couldn't he see how easily hurt I was and how his disapproval affected me?

I silently asked the Guys what I needed to do. *Sleep on it,* was their response. This meant apply the 24-Hour Rule and see how I felt in the morning. I knew it was up to me to change the dynamics between me and my dad, but how?

I woke up knowing what I had to do and fighting against it at the same time. I would have to talk with Dad about my feelings, after all, he couldn't change it if he wasn't aware there was an issue. At least that's what I told myself, but this understanding instilled fear. To no one in particular, I begged, *No, no, no. For the love of all that is holy, don't make me do that. Please! I'd rather publicly shit myself.* But there was no way around it. If I wanted to change this, heal this, then a heart-to-heart with my goliath of a dad was the only option.

I spent the next several minutes pacing the downstairs bedroom and mentally composing a frank, non-emotional and non-blaming dialogue. Finally, after many glances heavenward for help, I wiped the sweat off my palms, took a deep breath and headed up the stairs. I found Dad reading the newspaper and sipping his morning coffee.

He looked up, his brilliant blue eyes alert as ever, and said, "Good morning" as if nothing had transpired. This is how my family did anger. You blew up at someone, leaving them feeling like they'd stepped on a landmine and then you'd pretend all was right with the world. No apologies, no talking it through, just exploding, leaving the victim with gaping wounds and shrapnel, and then moving on. Dad's demeanor only confirmed for me that the cycle had to end.

I sat down, reached out my hand and caressed the top of his.

"Dad," I began softly. "I need to ask for your help with something."

He put the paper down and gave me his full attention. My lower lip started trembling. In an age-old attempt to self-soothe, I moved my hands to my lap where I nervously picked at my bitten nails and ripped cuticles.

I raised my eyes to his and with a shaky, strangled voice, said, "Dad. I didn't say what you thought I said last night. I'm sorry if what you thought I said hurt you. When you speak to me like that, I feel like a little girl again and I am frightened of you. I don't want that any longer so I'm gonna ask you not to talk to me like that again."

My dad, this amazing man who had survived so much, who had endured so much and would endure more, looked at me with genuine distress. His expression was that of a father who realized he had unintentionally caused his child anguish.

With knitted eyebrows and remorseful eyes, he said, "I'm sorry. I didn't know that. I'll work on it."

I reached out and lightly brushed the back of his hand. With my eyes on his and in a voice that was thick with emotion, I said, "Thank you, Dad."

True to his word, he never spoke to me that way again.

CHAPTER 36

Our little girl came to me in a dream. She was both frustrating and enchanting. Her blue eyes were so dark they appeared black. She effortlessly switched from being serious into peals of laughter. She was an enigma and I completely loved her.

It had been a while since Trinity and I had spoken about having children; in fact, during the previous months, he had made several sarcastic comments about getting another vasectomy. With the guidance of Susie and Rya, I realized he was trying to push my buttons and goad me into saying something that he viewed as manipulative or controlling, thereby justifying a second surgery. I refused to take the bait.

Whenever he said, "I'm so sick and tired of using condoms," I would ask, "What other birth control method were you thinking? I can't be on the Pill because it raises my blood pressure."

"I could have another vasectomy!" he'd quip snidely.

"Sure, Trinity. If you think that's best, go ahead. I can't support you, but it's your body."

Though I always kept my tone casual, my heart would be beating so fast I thought it would fly out of my chest.

As I've said before, Trinity was used to having women try to control him, so he was testing me, yet again, to see if I'd do the same.

Au contraire, mon chér. I'm not them and I'll never behave like them.

After putting it off for weeks, the dream was the incentive I needed. After inviting him over, and regardless of his mood, we were having the "children" talk. When he walked into my apartment and told me about his lousy day, my heart sank. I figured there was no way we could talk about this now, but the Guys had other ideas.

I had an epiphany (which is another word for divine intervention), that I should teach Trinity to meditate. When I asked him if he'd like to learn, I was surprised by his positive response. Without waiting for him to change his mind, I ushered him into the office and each of us found an inviting piece of carpeted flooring. We plopped down, he on his back and me on my hiney.

After making sure he was comfortable, I asked him to take a few deep, diaphragmatic breaths.

"Just listen to your breath flow in and out. That's all. That's where we start. Breathe in, breathe out."

"If I do too much of this, I'm gonna fall asleep."

I told him that would be okay. I stood, lit candles and started some New Age music. I then proceeded to lead him through an impromptu guided meditation. It didn't last long as I didn't want to overdo it. As I was finishing, I was guided to ask him if he'd like for me to give him Reiki and was again a bit surprised when he unhesitatingly replied, "Yes!"

Atta boy!

I hovered my hands above his heart and my sixth-sense lit up like the Fourth of July. I heard, *A child will be born of this union.*

Oh, no. Noooooo. No, NO! They didn't! Those sneaky little shits! The Guys knew I had an ethical standard which I strictly adhered to: I will not, in any way, judge or censor intuitive information.

In my head I snapped, *Come on, Guys! I am not telling him that. No frickin' way!*

Their matter of fact reply was: *If he were a client you would tell him. Tell him.*

They had me dead to rights, which elicited a wince.

I drew in a deep breath, opened an eye and peeked at Trinity, who appeared to be completely oblivious to my inner dilemma and narrative. I closed my eye, mentally crossed my arms and telepathically said, *No.*

Their response, a simple, *Yes.*

After going back and forth several times, I finally hissed, *You Guys be quiet and move on!* I suspected it wouldn't work, though. These pesky angels often won't leave me alone until I do as they've asked (yes, I had tested these waters before and it didn't work out so well for me). Still, I petulantly gave them the middle finger, a last-ditch effort to show my displeasure, then I resignedly took a deep breath and prepared for what might be the end of my relationship with Trinity.

Long ago, after watching Susie and other role models, I decided to be *very* real with my angels. That meant showing genuine emotion, personality and being forthright with my words. I think they love us even more because of it, after all, who knows us better than they do?

A case in point would be when Susie and I perform Reiki on each other. We are often so goofy that we receive strange looks from the Guys. Sometimes we howl with laughter at their stiff and overly formal speech and when they've overused the phrase, "be patient," we give them the stink eye. And when they urge us forward, we tell them that if they think this spiritual growth stuff is easy, then they should incarnate and give it a go. As always, the angels politely and patiently wait for us to finish and then they begin again.

These angels are not without humor, but they are usually all business. Every now and then when they want to tease Susie and me, they'll respond to a timeline question with the words, "Two weeks."

It is a reference to a point in time several years ago when Susie and I were both going through hell. Whenever we asked, "How much longer?!" the Guys would reply, *Two weeks.*

We would sigh in relief, thinking this nightmare would soon be over and that we'd be on the upswing. But, ooh *nooo.* At the end of those two weeks, it would go from bad to worse. Of course, we hadn't learned our lesson and would ask again, "How much longer?!" and they, in all seriousness, would reply, *Two weeks.* At the end of those two weeks, it would go from worse to hellish. Eventually we stopped asking and now "two weeks" is a running joke between us.

At the moment, as I looked down at Trinity's peaceful face, I was doing anything but laughing.

"Trin?" I said. "They are telling me I *have* to tell you something and I don't want to. I've fought them on this, but they are . . . insistent."

His eyes popped open and with a hint of concern he said, "Is there something physically wrong?" I shook my head no. "Well, what is it? Just tell me."

I repeated that I did not *want* to tell him. He asked why and I, eyes averted, softly mumbled that I was afraid and that I had a lot of fear surrounding this topic.

He tenderly said, "Why are you afraid? It's just me. Tell me."

"I'm afraid to tell you because I want what they are telling me with my entire heart."

I was caught between a solemn oath and a knowing that once I shared the information, he would have the power to take away my dreams. After sucking in another big breath, my fight, flight or freeze response kicked in. My heart was pounding, my mouth was dry, my hands were sweaty, and I just wanted to run away. In my head I threatened, *You Guys had better be right about this!*

My nervous eyes settled upon his wide and searching ones. I swallowed hard and in a whispered voice that was near tears said, "They are telling me that you and I will have a baby."

Then, not wanting to see his reaction, I clenched my eyes shut.

"A girl?" he asked.

My eyes popped open and found his. There was no malice or wariness in them, only honesty.

"Yes," I replied.

"The one you've seen?"

I nodded. He didn't say anything more and I didn't feel the need to press it.

Though my nerves were jangled, I continued to give him Reiki and intuitive information. When finished, I asked him, as I do with all my clients, if he had any questions or concerns.

"Nope. Nothing too frightening."

I almost fainted from relief.

CHAPTER 37

At some point, we had agreed that living apart was no longer what we wanted. Instead, and in this order, we wanted to buy a home, move in, become engaged and then marry. Trinity pre-qualified for the mortgage, then we searched for homes within our price range. We started by looking at bi-levels and I made the comment that they seemed so small.

Trinity agreed. "If we have a baby, we'd need more room."

He, of course, expected this comment to leave me speechless. I fooled him, though. I kept right on talking as if I hadn't heard him. With my mouth on autopilot, I tried to wrap my brain (and heart!) around his comment. Then, I halted mid-sentence and said, "Can we talk about what you were told during your Reiki session?"

"Oh, you mean about the baby thing?" he replied casually.

"Yup. Are you freaked out?"

"No. Not at all. If it happens it happens."

"Well, I'm *totally* freaked out," I sputtered. "Having a baby with you is something I want with all my heart. You *know* that! The more I love you, the more I want to have a baby with you. There's a reason I didn't want one with anyone else and there's a reason we haven't gotten pregnant yet; I'm not who I need to be, and neither are you."

Intent on making my statement clear, I narrowed my eyes. "If we are going to have a baby, there will be no mistake about the conception. It will be consensual and planned. You will never get the chance to say you weren't totally on board with bringing her into this world. If this happens, it's because we *both* agreed to it." Then, for good measure, I added, "And just so you know, I'm not leaving you. I want a baby with you so much I ache, but if you don't, if you are not one hundred percent committed, I will sacrifice having our little girl to be with you. I will *not* leave you."

In response, he gave me a boyish grin and said, "Didn't you hear what I said about the baby's room?"

Oh, I heard, buddy, I heard you loud and clear. But I also know how you have waffled in the past and I will not have any of that.

After blowing out a lungful of air and sharing a nervous smile, I confessed that the closer we got to having our dreams come true, the more afraid I became. I was fearful of returning to the unhappy and lonely person I was during my marriage and I didn't want him to turn into Ben. He admitted that he, too, was fighting old memories.

Having cleared that hurdle and confident we would soon find a house, we moved on to the topic of engagement rings. When Trinity asked if I wanted to be surprised by his choice, my reaction was one of mortification; my hand flew to my upper chest, my eyes went wide, and my mouth fell open.

"HELL NO!" I exclaimed. "I don't wanna wear a ring for the rest of my life that I don't absolutely love!" Then I realized what I must have sounded like and managed to reel it in. "While I love the idea of you picking it out on your own, it's not my vision. Can we do it together?"

"Yep! That's why I asked."

I pinched myself to see if I was dreaming.

CHAPTER 38

. . . Another blank page awaits for you. Does it surprise you to know that you have already filled up a page with your life? As you turn to this next clear, clean page, decide what it is that is really important to you – family, love, trust, et cetera. Write what you want, not what you do not want as you will only draw the negative to you should you choose that route. We tell you true, you can have it all . . . cars, money, fortune, fame and family. It all glides easily to you. Sit with that and when you put pen to paper, it will flow easily.

Your Other, your One, has firmly entered his core. He will not turn back or go back to the person he once was. He has evolved and transcended. He now shows others how it is done on the spiritual plane. His littlest one looks wholeheartedly at her daddy for guidance. Do you see how imperative it is that your Other remain in his core? To deviate could have disastrous results in the little eyes that are now upon him.

We do not wish to frighten, we wish for your Other to recognize his true power, his true potential. Your union is fated. You both have dreamed of this type of love and it occurs only once in a millennium. You two have found each other. Never lose sight of that.

Know that peace, beauty and bounty come to you both on swift wings. It is as it should be. All is happening for a reason and it will soon be made known to you both. We tell you there are a few tricks we will reveal but not before their time as they would lose their punch if we forewarned you. We smile at the wonder in your eyes for you see, you already know what is to happen. And you smile.

CHAPTER 39

As the house hunt continued, so did the search for the perfect engagement ring. After feeling frustrated by several failed outings, a bestie referred us to a local jewelry store where we found the perfect ring within a matter of minutes. Leaving the payment details – and the gem – until an undetermined later date, we left feeling as if everything was falling into place.

We had been planning a trip to Minot as Dad was having some health issues, including an agonizing pain in the upper right side of his back. A cortisone shot did nothing to alleviate it and he was having problems sleeping. What concerned me the most, though, was that he had given up his cherished golf game.

On our drive there, Trinity told me he wanted to ask my dad for permission to marry me.

"Don't you think that's a little archaic?" I asked, eyebrow arched. "I mean, we are both divorced and reestablished."

He shook his head. "No. It's a respect thing. It's a way that I can show your dad how much I love you. I want his blessing and if he asks us to wait, I will respect that."

I looked at him, incredulous. "You would *actually* wait if my dad asked you to?!"

"Yep. Totally."

Trinity and I arrived all smiles, but they quickly vanished when we opened the door to Dad's home. He was sitting in his normal spot, a stool at the kitchen counter. Except "sitting" is being too generous because he was so severely tilted, it looked as if he might topple over. As he turned his head to welcome us, it was clear he was very drunk. His words were slurred, and he was having trouble focusing his eyes.

All at once I became half little girl, half caretaker, both of which were on high alert and frozen with fear. With deadly calm, my wide eyes took in the situation and my brain started performing mental triage.

"Dad, are you okay?" I asked as my purse fell to the floor.

In a voice barely above a whisper, he said, "Awwwww, yeah. I'm just having a lot of pain, that's all."

As he was speaking, my body recognized there wasn't any imminent danger and thawed, allowing my legs to move. Because human touch is instinctual and as old as mankind, I lightly placed my hand on his arm. Searching his eyes, I tried to see what he wasn't saying. When I found it, the little girl in me vanished and the caretaker completely took over.

"Okay, Dad. How about I help you to bed. Will that be okay?"

He nodded and said, "I suppose that'd be alright."

Glancing over my shoulder, I saw Trinity standing in the doorway and sent him a look that conveyed I had this situation under control and he was not to help. Then I slid an arm around Dad's back and tried to help him stand. He placed a hand on the counter top and turned the stool so that both feet were in front of him. With them braced, and with my help, he corrected his angled posture and rose to his feet.

He was unsteady and looked as though he had shrunk five inches since I last saw him. His right shoulder blade hosted a visible egg-sized lump and sagged much lower than the left. Once my eyes saw the truth there was no unseeing it.

Please, God, I prayed. *Please let me keep it together in front of my dad. Don't let the tears come. Please. Not yet, okay?*

Taking our time, we walked through the dining room, then the hallway, and finally we reached the threshold of the bedroom he had shared with my mom. Turning to me and in an upbeat manner, he said, "Okay! I can take it from here."

I knew what he was saying; he wanted to undress without my help and maintain his dignity.

"Okay, Dad. Goodnight. Love you."

Having already turned away, he feebly replied, "Yup. Love you, too," as he shut the bedroom door.

Unable to wait until I heard the latch click, my face crumpled, and a flood of tears blurred my eyes. My face became hot and I gulped massive quantities of air as I whirled around, retraced my steps and raced towards the sanctuary I knew was waiting. Seeing me, my soon-to-be-fiancé opened his arms wide and I hurried into them, knowing the strength of his hug would grant me a temporary asylum.

He remained silent, kissing the top of my head, and holding me tightly as tears cascaded down my face. One thought echoed throughout my mind: *How did my dad, my larger-than-life dad, get old so quickly?*

CHAPTER 40

The next morning found Dad back to his spry, alert self. There were no signs of the withered, leaning man I had helped to bed the night before. Still, I knew Reiki would help so I asked him if he'd like to give it a try.

"Well, I don't see why not!" he replied.

Bless your heart, Dad.

Thankful for the foresight to bring the massage table with us, I asked Trinity to bring it in and set it up, something he did without hesitation.

With a pillow under Dad's head and a blanket over his torso, I explained what he might feel when I began. I told him about the phenomena of hands becoming as hot as heating pads. "You don't say!" was his chuckled response. After making sure he was comfortable, I inhaled and was immediately hit with a barrage of intuitive information. *Ooooooh, super!* I thought, and then almost shit a brick. I hadn't told my dad I saw and heard the deceased or that I was in constant contact with angels.

However, after the astral butt whoopin' I received from the Guys during Trinity's session, I knew better than to refuse.

Cringing and with a surrendering shrug, I thought, *Oh, what the hell. In for a penny, in for a pound.*

I lightly placed my hands on his shoulders and said, "Dad, you have a beautiful angel here. She's telling me her name is Gilda (meaning:

"Great Valor," something which suited my dad perfectly) and that she's been with you since birth. She's sooooo beautiful, Dad. She has long, silvery gray hair and is telling me that you want to return Home."

I paused and then asked, "Do you know what 'Home' means, Dad?"

He thought about it for a moment and then with uncertainty replied, "NoOOOooo." He ended the word with an uptick, as if it was a question. "Where are you getting your information from?"

Here we go!

"From guardian angels."

His eighty-three-year-old eyes widened. "Oh HO! Perhaps *you* should think about going to Jamestown."

Ha ha, Dad, very funny.

Jamestown is where the state mental hospital is located.

When I perform my work, people view me as an authority and I am careful not to abuse or deprecate that. Working on my dad was no exception, even in those early years. I may have giggled at his comment, but I didn't allow him to ignore what I had asked.

"Home" referred to Heaven, I told him and then asked, pointblank, "Dad. Are you afraid to die?"

He responded with an equally candid, "No."

Without speaking, I asked the Guys why Dad was still alive. They answered that he wanted to make sure all his children were properly taken care of. When I relayed this to my dad, he chuckled and downplayed it, but the proof was in the pudding. Later that day, when Trinity asked him for permission to marry me, Dad confided, "I worry about her. I just want to make sure she's taken care of."

The Guys told me my dad's heart was strong and he wouldn't die of a heart attack; in fact, that would be the last thing to give out or shut down. When I relayed this to Dad, he said he wasn't worried about that, what worried him was a stroke. I nodded and intuited that when he did die, he would be surrounded by those that he loved and who loved him. He would die peacefully and without pain.

I then heard that he saw my mom. When I asked him, he firmly denied it, "NO! I do *not*!"

Knowing my intuitive information was right, I didn't let his reply sway me. I repeated what I knew; that she was still with him and had just changed forms. I then raised one eyebrow and smugly said, "Oooooh, you see her all right, Old Man. You may not realize it or are afraid to say it, but you see her."

Amazingly, I was doing energy and intuitive work on a man who, even just a few years prior, would not have been open to this. A man who, at times, scared me more than any fictional boogieman and one that I had struggled to communicate with, even though he had brought my very existence into this world. When I worked on him, however, I didn't feel like a daughter or a caretaker anymore; I felt like a confident Healer and found I was equally as comfortable communicating validating information as I was delivering pure Reiki energy.

The fact that Dad had come so far in understanding and *accepting* both himself and me was key to becoming who I am today. To think, it could have all gone south if he had chosen to ridicule me or if I had shut down, but none of that happened. Instead, he embraced me and this newly-found Japanese energy work like a frickin' boss, helping me change my life – and then others – for the better.

One of the things I loved most about performing Reiki was the ability to see people for who they truly are. I stopped seeing one's external shell (i.e. tall, short, skinny or fat) and instead saw what was on the inside, their true form. I saw their fears and insecurities. I saw the hardships that they were trying to overcome as well as the injustices they had endured. I saw their strength, beauty, conviction, love and courage.

Even the people who had hurt me or that I did not like, when viewed through a spiritual lens, became a focus of my compassion. I knew what they were trying to overcome and how miserable or frightened they were trying to do so. In my personal life, I prayed for them and, sometimes telepathically let them know they could change.

When viewed in this light, even those who anger us or for whom we feel hatred are equally deserving of our forgiveness and understanding as those we love.

As I said earlier, each one of us is struggling to overcome; some will succeed, and others won't.

The night of his first Reiki treatment, my dad was in the same shape as when we first saw him. He had a high tolerance for physical pain, so when I noticed he was heavily self-medicating and was once again unable to sit upright, I *knew* that a whole bunch of bad was coming his way.

When I spoke to Dad about his death during the session, I was thinking he had maybe ten years left. The reality was closer to ten months. Within weeks, my dad would receive a diagnosis of stage four bone cancer. As he'd smoked for most of his life, it was believed that the cancer had originated in his lungs, then spread to his bones, where it tested his pain tolerance by producing fiendish agony. Within months, it would attack his brain. Dad would go Home shortly after celebrating his eighty-fourth birthday.

CHAPTER 41

A month after that visit, Trinity and I returned to Minot to see Dad again. During that time, shopping for a home had lost its appeal. After looking at nine million more bi-levels, Trinity was getting frustrated with the process, and with me as well. We found ourselves in another stalemate: I was adamant that we were to have a rambler and he was equally as insistent that we wouldn't find one within our price range. We needed some time away to overcome the impasse.

The morning after our arrival, Trinity was showering in the downstairs bathroom as I rounded the corner to go upstairs. At the base of the stairs was a big, plastic, neon-colored egg that stopped me dead in my tracks. Startled, I stared at it while something akin to panic built inside me.

Melissa, stop being a baby, I chided. I took a hesitant step and eyeballed the egg a little more. Another slow step followed by more staring and . . . I lost my nerve. Blowing out a breath, I turned and walked away, muttering the word "shit" as I did.

What a conundrum. On one hand, I was pee-my-pants excited at the prospect of my engagement ring being inside and on the other, scared silly because that plastic egg may just contain a symbol representing big changes. Exciting changes, yes, but big changes nonetheless. I turned and walked towards the stairs again. As I suspected, the egg was still there. Nervously, I started jumping up and down like a kangaroo on steroids. My hands remained clutched at my chest and my wide eyes never left the brightly colored egg.

Oh, for pity's sake, Melissa. Grow a set!

I bent down and with shaky hands retrieved the egg and carried it upstairs.

"Hummm," I said as I carefully set it down in front of my dad. "It appears the Easter Bunny left me an egg."

Dad's eyes widened, and he smiled. "I guess he did!"

I left the egg exactly where I had placed it, poured a cup of coffee and waited for Trinity to finish his shower. Was it just my lifelong aversion to patience, I wondered, or was Trinity taking a ridiculous amount of time? When I couldn't stand it another second, I raced down the stairs and flung open the bathroom door.

"Hey, hon?" I managed casually. "Yeah, ummmm, should I open this egg without you?"

He cheerily perked, "Absolutely!"

Whaaaa? I certainly wasn't expecting that.

Shutting the bathroom door, I retraced my steps, this time taking the stairs two at a time and I didn't slow down until I reached the kitchen counter. As my dad watched, I grabbed the egg and twisted it open, simultaneously relieved and disappointed when I saw not a ring but a tiny handmade card. The words, scrawled by my Other, brought tears to my eyes.

I heard the shower shut off and instinctively knew something big was about to go down. Taking the stairs at a much more casual pace, I walked into the bathroom and with a hug and a kiss thanked him for the card.

He smiled and said, "There's more eggs to find!"

My eyes lit up.

I had always loved Easter egg hunts and looked forward to them each year. When one Easter Sunday I woke up to find that the Easter Bunny "forgot" to hide the eggs, I was beyond upset and let everyone in the house know it before storming from the kitchen. And wouldn't you know it, while I was fuming in my bedroom, the Easter Bunny made an emergency visit.

With Trinity near, I joyfully started hunting for more eggs and before long found the second. Would this be "the one?" I cautiously opened it and found it contained a Hershey's Kiss. Sort of anticlimactic, but it was chocolate so still a win in my eyes.

The third contained a Rolo. Chocolate *and* caramel, even better, but still no ring. By the fourth egg I was getting rather blasé about the whole deal. I found I wasn't holding the egg like it was a precious chrysalis anymore, nor was I squealing and squishing my eyes shut each time I opened one. No, by the time the fourth egg was found, I was expecting another sweet treat, so I unceremoniously wrenched it open. Turned out the *yoke* was on me. Instead of chocolate or caramel, egg number *cuatro* contained my engagement ring.

Obviously, I was caught off guard. My mouth fell to my knees and if the carpet hadn't been glued to the floor, I would have inhaled it. I went from indifference to astonishment quicker than you could say, "Slap my ass and call me Judy." And when Trinity dropped to one knee, I was even more unnerved. Jogging in place, I let out a high-pitched squeal.

Trinity was nervous. His hands were trembling, and I could tell his mouth was dry. I had stopped my imitation of a prancing pony and began clapping like a circus seal while rapidly chanting "Oh my God" in ascending decibels. Despite that, he looked at me and said, "Melissa. Will you marry me?"

"YAAAAAAAS!" I shouted, and my clapping switched to a spasmodic version of jazz hands.

When Trinity stood, I attempted to regain a modicum of composure. My flailing quieted as he reached for my left hand and placed the ring on my finger. I held out my hand, momentarily admiring the stunning gem, and then our eyes met. With smiles that would make Julia Roberts proud, we hugged. As we pulled away, the smiles, while gone from our faces, remained in our eyes and we kissed deeply and passionately.

When we pulled apart, I looked at my ring again and the mega-watt smile returned. It really was a perfect thing of beauty. Holding hands, we climbed the stairs to share the news with my dad.

"Dad!" I shouted as if he hadn't known what was going on. "We're engaged!"

My dad's face broke into a smile. "Congratulations!" he said, as he first shook my fiancé's hand and then enveloped me in a hug.

CHAPTER 42

It was another typical Sunday in late April and I really, really didn't want to go look at another house. Even though Trinity had assured me this would be the last one for a while, my mood remained sour. Pulling into the driveway of a newly built rambler, I was not impressed. It was so . . . *pedestrian.* There was nothing special or magical about it, and I was even more annoyed when Trinity said he wanted to go in and look around.

"What a colossal waste of my time," I sniped when he was out of earshot.

Imagine my surprise, and subsequent chagrin, when we discovered this was the house we'd been waiting for, had fights over and had begun worrying wouldn't materialize. This house, complete with a sun room and a three-stall garage, was the physical embodiment of our wish lists. And because it fit both our budget and needs, we agreed to put in an offer immediately. The builder responded favorably, and within an hour of walking through the front door, we were under contract.

Pah pow!

The realtor commented that the house had been on the market since January and hadn't had many showings. This surprised us, but not as much as his disclosure the next day. Upon meeting us at our soon-to-be home for a closer inspection, the realtor shared that two more purchase offers had come in overnight.

Melissa Schaff

Sorry, folks, this house was waiting for us.

Citing a new home as the motivation, Trinity, a tobacco chewer since age fourteen, decided it was time to break the self-soothing habit. Unfortunately (for me), he chose to do it, not by weaning himself off, but by going cold turkey . . . on the day of our move. In this case, his strong German heritage worked to his advantage; he did quit. I, however, lost more than a pound of flesh, but considered myself lucky as I lived to tell the tale.

Shortly after settling in, we decided we wanted to get married on August 8. It was a day rich in symbolism for us, as the number eight flipped on its side is the infinity symbol. Another, more practical, reason was Trinity had a work trip scheduled for early September and I wanted to be married prior to that.

Trinity and I had church weddings the first time around, and now we wanted something different. We decided to get married at the campsite where he had told me that he loved me, but we couldn't figure out the logistics of getting our families there. As it turned out, that didn't matter.

Late one evening, I had another epiphany: Susie needed to marry us. It was so perfect I was surprised I hadn't thought of it before. When I asked Trinity how he felt about that idea, he said he was all-in. Then I suggested we get married in Susie's backyard and that was also a go. When I asked Susie, who was an online ordained minister, if she would do the honors she agreed without hesitation. That left selecting a witness and there was never any doubt that Rya would fill that role. In many ways, both she and Susie had taken this journey with us.

We wanted a casual and very small wedding, and so we invited only my immediate family. Dad regretfully declined due to reduced upper body mobility that made driving – or riding - nearly impossible. That left my brother and sister. And then, exactly what I didn't want to happen, happened. After receiving feedback that a local relative might feel slighted if not invited, I rescinded my siblings' invitations. It was an even smaller affair than we had wanted, but it was perfect.

Under a beautiful tree that emanated strength and resilience and physically sheltered us from a light drizzle, one of my besties stood beside me and the other one in front of me. These two amazing women had been through it all with me. They were there when I saw threes everywhere and when I was repulsed by Trinity and later infatuated with him. They were there when we started dating and talked me down from the proverbial ledge when he ended our relationship.

They provided invaluable spiritual insight as well as spoke the cold, hard truth when I needed to hear it. They were my protectors when Trinity came back into my life and my soul-soothers when I feared he would leave it again. They laughed with me and cried for me. I could not have done any of this without their unyielding support, strength and unconditional love.

When I said "I do" to my forever husband, their presence was the ideal ending to the dating diaries and the perfect beginning of the marriage story.

CHAPTER 43

In the months that followed our wedding, Dad's uncontrolled cancer continued to greedily consume everything in its path. Without treatment, which Dad had decided against, the doctors told him his condition would only continue to worsen.

Despite their opinion, I was insistent that his cancer diagnosis was a false one.

"Dad, you do *not* have cancer. I see white spots. Cancer shows up black."

By this time he was used to, and understood, my extrasensory lingo. He calmly, firmly and yet somehow gently said, "Melissa. I do have cancer. It *is* cancer."

God in heaven. He's acknowledging it, he's given it a name. He's owning this disease. Shiiiiit! That makes it real.

I left that conversation feeling shaken and confused. *He can't,* I thought. *He can't have cancer! The Guys said it wasn't cancer and they are never wrong. So, what in the holy hell is this about?!*

Immediately, I took my fear and channeled it into anger. And, of *course*, I aimed it at my guardian angels. *You Guys told me just two weeks ago that my dad did* not *have cancer. Clearly, he does. CLEARLY! What the fuck, Guys? Why would you deceive me? Why would you tell me he doesn't when he does!?*

A clear voice, free of any animosity or unkindness said, *He does not have cancer, little one. The medical community does not know what to call it, so they choose to say it is cancer.*

That took the wind right out of my sails. *Uhhhh,* I thought as I processed their words and then once understanding dawned, *Oooooh.*

In a small, much humbler voice, I asked, *Well, what is it then?*

The distinct, strong voice replied, *It is not of your world. It is something undiscovered. When the medical world cannot figure out what something is, they label it as cancer.*

My lips formed a small O in understanding. Western medicine is still in its infancy, and while we have many advancements to be thankful for, there is still much to discover.

"Thank you, Guys!" I said out loud, and I meant it. Not only had what they shared helped me move forward, it also helped me understand that I was not wrong in my knowing. My dad did *not* have cancer, but the outcome would be the same as if he did.

As my dad's physical life was coming to an end, Trinity's and my married life was just beginning. As with most newlyweds, there were adjustments to make and trials to work through. While most of these were minor, a major source of our stress came from Trinity's ex-wife and, sometimes, their son. The smiling and gregarious little boy I had previously met was gone, replaced by a wary and withdrawn eight-year-old who had become very good at emotional compartmentalization.

I had earlier glimpsed Ian's light and understood that his greatest gift would be his unending kindness. For that, and so many other reasons, I loved this sweet little boy and welcomed the chance to help raise him. But, in order to do that, I needed him to know that I wasn't leaving, he belonged here, and I was trustworthy.

In addition to these issues, we had extrinsic hurdles to overcome. During the first year of our marriage, Ian was often disrespectful and would sometimes ignore me. At one point, he glared at me and sneered, "Why is *she* even here?"

Trinity, quick to correct this behavior, said I was a part of his life and therefore a part of Ian's as well. I wasn't going anywhere, and Ian needed to show me more respect.

As if I wasn't in the room, Ian replied, "Mom told me to ignore her. She also said Melissa won't be around long so I shouldn't get attached."

I knew Ian's mom was using bitterness to cover up unhealed emotional wounds. I saw both her beauty and her fears and prayed she'd find the strength to leave the past behind and move forward. And because I saw these things, at first, I greeted comments like this with compassion. However, as time went on it became more and more difficult.

I reached my limit when her nasty grams repeatedly brought me to tears. She reminded me far too much of all the abuse – and the abusers - I had struggled to be rid of.

And still, I prayed she'd find her (spiritual) way.

CHAPTER 44

My siblings and I had decided to take turns staying with Dad since he wanted to remain in his home as long as possible. Daily, we reported what we saw via phone or group email, and it wasn't long before our differences in perception showed themselves. For instance, I am an eternal optimist, a real glass-half-full cheerleader. In truth, I held out hope that my dad would rally and get better, right up until the moment he took his last breath. My sister gravitated toward the other end of the spectrum and my brother was somewhere in the middle; if I saw white, my sister saw black and my brother saw gray.

Though I wouldn't have missed that time with my dad for anything, I found myself torn between my two families. Sometimes my turn with Dad fell on a Tuesday or a weekend, which were the days Trinity and I had Ian. Viewing those times as sacred, I felt deeply conflicted and often cried if I was away. I had even given up my Tuesday night golf league so I could spend time with Ian. Trinity reassured me I was doing the right thing, and while I agreed with him that I needed to be with my dad it still bothered me terribly. What I was feeling was no different than any parent trying to make sure everyone they cared for felt loved.

In the hope of shrinking the now baseball-sized tumor and give him some relief from the relentless agony, Dad agreed to have radiation therapy. This caused his skin to react as if it had been burned. Gently rubbing the soothing aloe balm into the blistered area, I noticed how my dad's once hale and hearty body was now bordering on emaciation. His tumor had interfered with his dexterity and he was no longer able to write with his dominant hand. Since his arm was virtually useless, he had taken to wearing it in a sling, which served not only as a visual reminder to keep it immobile but also to prevent the stabbing jolts of misery if he forgot.

Throughout all of this, I had been giving Dad Reiki. One morning, as I emerged from the basement, he turned to me and with amazement said, "You know? I think Reiki is really helping my pain!"

Fist pump!

"That's SO *great*, Dad!"

The memory of why I got into Reiki came back to me and I smiled, knowing I *had* helped him.

While Dad appreciated all that his kids were doing, he also worried that he was becoming a burden.

"Melissa. I feel badly that you are coming home so often. You are just married and are trying to run a business and a household. I'm fine here."

The old me would have let the Old Man have this one as I grew up in an era where children "should be seen and not heard." But the new me had grown and I felt inspired by his love. With tears forming, I reached across the counter and touched his hand.

"Dad, I want to do this for you. You raised me. You fed me, you clothed me, and you did your Goddamn best to teach me right from wrong. I want to honor you. I want to be a part of this. I *want* to be here. I want to care for you and try to repay you for all the years you took care of me."

By this time crocodile tears were falling freely down my cheeks. My dad, uncomfortable with tears or maybe just those of his youngest daughter, turned his head away. When he did so, I caught a glimpse of unshed tears in his eyes.

"I *need* to do this," I continued, as I fought for control of my emotions. "You are my dad and without you I wouldn't even be here. I wouldn't be alive." Then, losing the battle, my voice broke. "Please, *please*, Dad. Let me show you the respect and honor you deserve by helping you however I can."

When he replied, his voice was thick with emotion, so different from the man I'd known all my life, but in typical Dad fashion he got right to the point.

"Well," he said with a single nod of his head, "I guess that's okay then."

I left my seat and walked to him. As I did so, I smile-cried. It wasn't possible to love him more than I did at that moment. Intent on showing it, but being mindful of his incapacitated and painful shoulder, I gently gave him a version of a crushing hug.

CHAPTER 45

Over the next few months, I watched as my dad took his fate in stride. He didn't complain, he didn't throw a pity party, he just accepted it. I continued to give him Reiki as often as possible, even if it was just for five minutes, because as my former students know, any Reiki is better than no Reiki. He continued to tell me he thought it was helping diminish the pain. I, however, was secretly hoping it was curing his "cancer" even though I knew this went against Dad's desires.

He was tired, he said, and didn't want to beat this disease. He'd buried his parents, his wife and all but one of his four siblings. He had fought in a war, raised three morally and ethically responsible children (no small feat) and attended many of his best friends' funerals. Simply put, he didn't want to be on earth anymore.

One morning, while sipping coffee in my Fargo kitchen, I received a call from my sister.

"Dad fell!" she exclaimed. "He was trying to reach your Goddamn chokecherry syrup and he fell. He's in the hospital."

She's pissed at me because I brought dad chokecherry syrup and because he fell trying to get it? She's blaming me? What the fuck? I paused a beat, then thought, *Stress does strange things to people.*

"I'll be there in five hours."

Thankfully Dad hadn't broken anything, but he was starting to lose coordination. It was the beginning of the end, a fact I remained glass-half-full unaware. Still, as I drove, I cursed the distance between

Fargo and Minot and pushed the pedal down as far as I felt I could get away with. Long ago, when I traveled for a living, I had struck a deal with God: "You let me speed on my way there (anywhere) and I'll obey the limits on my return trip." That deal had worked well for me over the years, and it did that day too.

Another traveling trait, which I had gotten from my dad, was a refusal to stop while on the road. By the time I arrived at the hospital my bladder was near bursting and I raced to the closest women's bathroom. After taking care of business, I found my dad's room and what I saw when I entered stopped me dead in my tracks. Dad was sitting on the side of the bed looking out of the third-floor window. His view was not soothing greenery but concrete, tar and traffic. His hospital gown was tied at the back and his hands were braced on either side of his thighs. His fingers were tapping out the same rhythm he had unconsciously played for a lifetime.

Sometimes being a practicing intuitive and Empath isn't enjoyable, in fact, it can be downright painful. While these abilities have always been useful, each carries its own curse as well. As I stood in the doorway, I knew my dad was thinking that this was officially a one-way street, and that he'd never golf again. On the heels of that, came a sense that he had given up and was resigned to dying.

My heart caught in mid-beat and my breath stilled. I blinked rapidly, trying to come to terms with this knowledge. Then, after a calming breath, I faked a perky, "Dad! What in the hell, Old Man? What happened?"

Upon hearing my voice, his upper body twisted towards me while his eyes, showing no trace of what I had just intuited, found mine. He smiled, lifted an eyebrow and said, "Well, hello! When did you get here?"

During the morning hours, Dad was lucid and talkative, but later in the day, as his pain grew, he was barely cognizant and faded in and out of morphine-induced sleep. I knew from previous talks that Dad wanted to die in his home, so when he asked me if he would get out of the hospital and return there, I answered honestly, "I don't know, Dad. We'll have to see."

On the third day, Dad wasn't eating; however, while he may have lost his appetite, his notorious sweet tooth was very much intact. He agreed to try a milkshake, and as I was holding it for him and encouraging him to have more, a memory surfaced, and with it, some tears. Years after Mom died, I was pushing him to eat more, much like I was now, when he raised an eyebrow and with a quizzical smile asked, "Melissa? How on earth did I survive all this time without you?"

Without missing a beat, I'd replied, "That's a good question, Dad."

By this time, Dad was shaking badly and unable to sit up unassisted, so I offered him the use of my back as a support for his. As the two of us sat there, facing opposite directions, he let his feet dangle off the bed as he sipped the chocolate shake and once again stared outside at the bleak landscape.

Setting the container aside, his fingers found the portable bedside tray and broke the comfortable silence by drumming out a familiar tune. I smiled with sadness.

"I'm gonna miss that, Dad."

"Miss what?"

"I'm gonna miss how you absently drum your fingers and jangle the change in your front pants pocket. I'm gonna miss how you sort of whistle but more blow when you are concentrating on fixing something. Nobody does it like you, Dad. I'm gonna miss all that stuff."

He genially quipped, "Oh! Is that right?"

Then I decided to tackle a question that had caused me psychological discomfort for decades. Having repeatedly heard from my brother and sister that I was an "oops" and they had been planned, I realized I equated being unplanned with being unwanted or "less-than."

"Dad? Was I planned?"

Without missing a beat, he replied, "Yes!" thus healing, with one word, some of my emotional damage.

"Did you and Mom want more kids?"

He waggled his hand and said, "Oh, if it happened, it happened."

Staying past visiting hours, I listened as Dad talked unintelligibly in his morphine sleep. Reverting to my childhood and proving, once again, old habits die hard, I couldn't bring myself to leave him, not even to use the restroom or grab a bite to eat. The book I'd brought with me, normally engaging, now failed to hold my attention and I put it aside and instead spent long intervals watching him doze. When I noticed his shrunken, frail body was shaking like an aspen leaf, I asked, "Dad? Are you cold?"

"Yeah, a little."

"Okay. Let me get a nurse and we'll get you warmed up."

Within minutes of my pressing the call button, a nurse arrived. I could tell this wasn't her first cancer circuit rodeo and I appreciated that. With knowing eyes, she calmly assessed my dad and then looked at his chart.

"It's been awhile since his last morphine. Let me get a doctor to authorize some more. I'm also going to get him a heated blanket."

Filled with gratitude, I met her eyes, smiled and thanked her.

Then, having learned an unforgettable lesson a decade before, I did what felt right; I crawled on top of the covers and spooned my dad, just as I had wanted to do with my mom. The old me would have felt awkward but the new me didn't give a rat's ass. My dad was dying, and his shivers looked like spasms; I knew my body heat would help. A part of me knew, and tried to block out, that his tremors weren't only from being cold, but also from the relentless pain.

"I'm here, Dad. I'm here. Lemme help you. A warm blanket and more morphine are on their way. Until then, let's see what we can do to get you warm."

I gingerly rubbed his blanketed arm, torso, hip and finally, his spaghetti-thin legs. When finished, I curled my small frame into his slightly larger one and held him.

Noticing his breath was shallow and rapid, I murmured, "It's okay, Dad. Just breathe. I'm here. You're fine. It's gonna be fine. Just breathe. Take in some deep, slow breaths, okay? Let them expand your tummy and then exhale."

Pausing to rub his arm again, I looked at his drawn, ashen face, and then continued. "I'm here, Daddy. You're not alone. Can you feel me, Dad? Can you feel the heat from my hands and the warmth of my hug? It's okay, Dad. It's okay. You're okay. You're safe. I'm here. Breathe, Dad. Just breathe."

Returning with the warm blanket and the morphine-filled syringe, the nurse draped the blanket over both of us, and then injected the medicine into his IV tube. Within minutes the tremors had subsided and he lightly dozed. Feeling like my body heat was no longer needed, I exited the bed, used the restroom and returned to my chair. After glancing at Dad, I lowered my head and opened my book, intent upon losing myself in it.

But before I could do so, an almost imperceptible movement caught the corner of my eye. My head snapped upward, and my eyes landed at the foot of the bed where a breathtakingly handsome archangel stood. His shirtless seven-foot frame had jet black shimmering wings which were spread out on the wall behind him. His loosely crossed, muscular arms rested on his rugged chest. His lower body was clad in black leather, his feet, one of which was resting against the wall, were housed in black, thick-soled and knee-high leather boots.

And while all of that was spectacular, it was his face that captured – and held - my attention. It was that of an Adonis, with an alabaster complexion, a strong chiseled jaw, a perfectly formed Greek nose and full, sensuous, red-tinged lips. Highly sculpted cheekbones sat beneath intelligent obsidian eyes, those being rimmed with long, thick, black lashes. And finally, a mass of wavy, thick black hair fell about his shoulders. Never had I seen such a perfectly formed or handsome visage.

Had I stared at him one moment more, I would have unabashedly wept at his ethereal exquisiteness.

Neither his body, height, nor demeanor were frightening, but it was Hollywood's evil depiction of black that caused me to erroneously conclude he was there to harm my dad. Had I been less quick to judge, I might have realized he could never do as I feared because he emanated restraint, compassion, and respect.

As it was though, I transformed into something decidedly feral. I stood, lowered my head, bared my teeth and glared at him.

You are not welcome here, I telepathically snarled. *You need to leave. NOW!*

Then, like a petulant child willing a monster to be gone, I squished my eyes shut. Seconds later, unable to take the suspense, I opened them. To my delight, the archangel had complied with my demand; he was gone.

Quickly, I pivoted my head around the room, surveying it. If he was still there, I was ready for battle. Seeing no sign of him, not even that of his energetic presence, I remained in a crouched stance while I gave one last cursory glance. Then, having deemed it safe, I stood to my full height and thought, *Good Lord, Melissa. Anyone passing by would think you're a crazy lady.*

My entire body was shaking, and I thought I might collapse, but I managed to turn toward my still dozing dad. Immediately, my warring energy melted away. With the back of my hand, I touched his brow, and then lightly kissed his drawn, cool cheek.

"I love you, Dad," I whispered. "I'll be back tomorrow."

With that, I hauled ass out of the hospital room, all the while internally bitching, *What in the FUCK, Guys?! What in the FUCK?! You're supposed to protect me. That's the deal. I do this work and you protect me. What in the FUCK was that all about?!*

No response was received.

When I returned early the next morning, Dad was his old self again, complete with a dry sense of humor. Just after we had chuckled about whether he could get some gin, a staff member entered and, without any small talk, said, "You're moving to a nursing home today."

Instantly, the smiles fell from our faces, his body wilted, and my shoulders sagged. Clearly, we both had held out hope that he could go home, but with untreated, end-stage cancer, this was not going to happen. Knowing this was coming, we kids had looked into options but decided a nursing home was, unfortunately for our dad, the only choice.

Still, it crushed me when his searching eyes found mine and he asked, "Can't I go home?"

"No, Dad," I said while exhaling. "None of us kids can take care of you there. We aren't strong enough to help you out of bed or to use the bathroom." Tears burned my eyes and my voice cracked, "I'm so sorry, Daddy."

My dad's eyes left mine and landed on the floor as he processed this, and when he slowly raised them, they were filled with desperation and vulnerability.

"Why haven't I died yet?"

This unanswerable question broke my heart and I swallowed hard. Unable to keep it together, my face began to crumble just as the ambulance crew entered the room. Uncomfortable with others seeing the rawness of my emotions, and not wanting to create a scene, their entrance stopped me from falling to the ground and sobbing out the unfairness of it all. If this scenario had happened today, I would have done just that and to hell with anyone's discomfort.

Through tears that sometimes obscured the traffic lights, I followed the ambulance in a state of shock as it transported my dad to the nursing home. After drying my tears, I entered the building and instantly despised the wretched place. It smelled like urine, antiseptic and death.

Buckle up, buttercup.

We had reserved a private room but upon arrival were told one wasn't available yet. *Sooooo*, I thought, *are we waiting for some poor guy to die, or what?* In the interim, Dad was placed in a double occupancy unit. As Dad entered the room, he walked to the empty bed and sat dispiritedly on its side. He took a deep breath, and as he let it out, his head fell forward, and his shoulders slumped. Consumed with remorse and grief, I looked away but not before tears filled my eyes.

Within minutes, the nurse came to do an evaluation. When asked if he knew who the young lady was sitting next to him, I held my breath and prayed, *Please God. Please let my dad remember me.* This was ridiculous, of course, as he hadn't suffered any memory loss, but that's where my mind went.

My dad looked at me and said, "Yes. That's my daughter, Melissa."

With an audible whoosh, I released my breath.

"That's *right*, Dad!" I said, as if he had just completed a great feat.

As the nurse finished, I told Dad I needed to return to Fargo but I'd be back that weekend. He nodded, thanked me and then I gently hugged and kissed him goodbye. As I walked out of the room, I heard him introduce himself to his roommate.

That's so my dad, I thought, proudly. And then I burst into tears.

Less than twelve hours after my return to Fargo, I received a call from the nursing home telling me it wouldn't be much longer. After refueling the car, I started my somber drive and began a one-sided conversation with Dad.

"Dad. It's okay. You can go without me being there. You don't need to wait for me. Just go, Dad. Go! I'm there in spirit already. Can you feel me?"

Unable to hold back the tears any longer, I sobbed, "You don't have to wait for me to get there, Daddy. If you're in pain, if you wanna go, then please go. Don't wait for me."

But he did wait, and within minutes of my bedside arrival, he took his last breath.

Upon entering his room, I saw my brother and sister flanking his bed. Dad's eyes were closed, and he was breathing with the help of a machine. I walked to the head of the bed, stroked his forehead and looked at him lovingly. Then I slid my arm under his neck and repeatedly butterfly-kissed his forehead. I wanted to lay with him, as I had in the hospital, but the bed was too small. Improvising, I sat on it, as close to him as I could manage, and caressed his arms, face, and chest.

I whispered, "Dad. It's okay to go. We're all here. I made it, Dad. You waited for me. Thank you. But if you're ready, Daddy, it's okay to leave."

A snippet of what the Guys had earlier said about his death returned to me: *He will be surrounded by those who love him.*

With that, I let the brimming tears fall as my eyes left Dad's face and swept over his body. When they reached his toes, I saw the same archangel again. This time, however, he stood upright, his shoulders were straight, head was bowed, feet were firmly planted, and his hands were loosely clasped in front of him. Once again, he emanated strength and power, but also sorrow and humility. Because of that, and the fact that he was clearly mourning with us, I didn't feel threatened or protective.

Instead, I saw with clarity that his earlier presence was merely to check on Dad's progress. Now, it meant he would escort my dad Home.

Returning my gaze to Dad's face, I saw that it had become even paler. I placed one hand on his chest and felt the steady tempo of his heartbeat. *His heart will be the last to go,* emerged from my memory banks, yet another fragment of angelic conversation. Telepathically, I repeated, *It's okay, Dad. Go. There's an angel here to help you. Do you see him? I love you, Daddy. I love you so very much.*

At that point I kissed his brow again, letting my lips linger. He felt colder. Keeping my hand on his chest, I raised my head and looked towards the foot of the bed again. This time I not only saw the archangel but a much younger and see-through version of Dad. The archangel stood slightly behind and to the side of my dad, who was wearing a black suit with a thin black tie, a crisply ironed white shirt, and appeared to be in his early fifties. His hair was darker, his face less lined, and his build slimmer. Like the archangel, he had adopted a stance of respectful mourning.

I glanced back at the body my dad's soul had inhabited for eighty-four years. He was no longer there; his strong heart had quit beating beneath my hand. Again, I looked at the astral version of my dad and as I did so, a somber but peaceful smile formed on my lips and tears streamed down my cheeks. I was overcome with relief that my dad was no longer in agony and that he was going somewhere where there were lots of fabulous golf courses.

I also knew that while his pain had ended, ours had just begun. I looked at my siblings, newly orphaned like me, and saw that their heads were bowed; they were unaware of the grandeur I was seeing. Never had I taken so much comfort in, or felt so blessed by, my gifts.

Once again, I returned my gaze to the semi-transparent version of my dad. I kept willing him to look up, but he didn't. He stayed as he was until both he and the archangel faded from view. When I could no longer see him, I panicked and called out, *Dad?! DAD! I love you! Please let me know when you've made it.*

About five months after his death, Trinity and I were camping at our favorite campground. Wanting to be alone, I declined Trinity's offer to join him fishing. The campground was quiet, a rarity, but it was exactly as I liked. The bugs were biting someone else and as the sun set, I opened my first beer, grabbed a book and sat in a chair by the unlit firepit. Intent on enjoying a few minutes of tranquility and the sun's warmth, I closed my eyes, letting my head rest on the back of the seat.

Minutes passed when something, possibly a noise or a smell that didn't belong, broke through the reverie. I lifted my head and opened my eyes. There, about five feet away from me, was my dad, smiling and sitting on a log with his arms dangling off his bent knees and fingers holding a half-smoked cigarette. He was wearing hideous red and pink checkered golf shorts from the late seventies and a white golf shirt. Despite his clothes, I thought, *Damn!* The Old Man looks good!

My eyes drank in his tanned, healthy face and I noticed that his blue eyes seemed even more vivid. There wasn't any sign of the ravages of cancer and, as before, he appeared to be about thirty years younger than when he passed.

My face split into a smile. *Hi Daddy!*

Ever a man of few words, he said, *Well, you asked me to tell you when I made it. I made it. So, I guess that's it.* Almost as an afterthought he added, *I'll bring your mother with me next time.*

My smile grew broader at his brevity, and with my eyes glued to his beloved face I said, *Okay, Daddy. I love you.*

Yep. Guess I love you, too. Well, I'm off then. And without further ado, he vanished.

I stared at the spot he had briefly occupied and felt eternally grateful. With a smile still lingering, I closed my eyes and discovered the feelings of sorrow and loss were being replaced with comfort and peace.

CHAPTER 46

My relationship with Susie had already evolved from client to friend when, many years ago, a group of us students performed Reiki on her. As I hovered my hands above her heart, I felt as if I was going to cry a river. Determined not to second guess this or be quieted by intimidation, I blurted, "Oooh, Suuuuuusie."

Her eyes popped open and she raised her head. Looking directly at me, she grabbed both of my hands and held them in hers, then burst into tears.

My leap of faith had assisted Susie in healing an old wound. Unfortunately, she had developed a history of being taken advantage of by people she trusted, and with me, that didn't happen. We decided to give each other Reiki on a regular basis and while doing so, our bond strengthened, allowing us to share our fears, secrets and, as I said earlier, laughter.

Because of this openness, Susie understood, perhaps even more than my forever husband, just how much I wanted a child with him. Unwaveringly, she would tell me I'd get pregnant with an egg released from my right ovary and that it would be a girl. She cautioned me to prepare as the baby would be a queen without a throne and would arrive ready to rule. I would ask, "Can I handle her? Can I do this?!" and she would reply that I could, or the baby would have chosen different parents.

After sharing this information with Trinity and occasionally saying, "Honey, I really want to give birth to your little girl," he would mumble,

"I'm not ready to try." Because of that, we continued faithfully using birth control. And when Susie would tell me I would be pregnant in a given number of months, and it didn't happen, I would shrug it off. After all, the odds of a safe sex pregnancy were slim to none.

However, after months of these conversations – and after celebrating another birthday – I became anxious. Even though I consoled myself with the old adage, *If it's meant to be, it'll be,* I knew time was not on my side.

One night, Trinity and I were having dinner at one of our favorite restaurants. Looking up from his plate, and in a voice that was barely above a whisper, he said, "I think we should try."

Trying to process his words, I stared blankly at him, head tilted and mouth open. As butterflies took flight in my stomach, I wanted to run but my legs wouldn't obey. What had he just said? Accessing my memory bank, my eyes drifted from his. We should try . . . *for a b . . . ba . . . baby?!* Sensing deceit, my eyes narrowed and returned to his, searching. Not finding anything amiss, I then scoured his face, looking for his signature teasing smile but found only honesty.

Why hasn't he said he's kidding? I wondered.

Because he wasn't.

"What?" I managed to sputter. "Are you kidding me?!"

"No. I've been thinking about this for a while and I think it's time we try."

"Are you *kidding* me," I repeated, "because this isn't funny if you are. Are you?"

His eyes were full of love as he reached across the table and grabbed my hand. "No. I'm not kidding. I think we should try."

Fuuuuuuuck.

Hyperventilating, I said, "Oh my God! Trinity! I think I'm gonna pass out."

Looking at him with wonder, tears swam in my eyes. He stroked my fingers slowly, allowing me to calm down, and when I did, I asked one final time, "Really?"

"Really."

Server? Check, please!

Each time we made love, I wondered with excitement if I would become pregnant. And each time Mother Nature showed me I was not, I became disappointed. As the months passed, I started to resent and dread Aunt Flo's visit. Her crimson appearance would cause me to slide to the bathroom floor where, in a heap, I would sob.

By this stage of my life, my body and I were old friends and I knew her well. For as long as I could remember, I had experienced painful left side ovulations because the egg traveled over a fallopian tube cyst. Now, trusting that a baby would come from an egg released from the right ovary, I was not vested in getting pregnant during the left-side months. I wasn't counting my fertility days, nor was I viewing sex as a means to an end. Instead, and like it should be, I was playful and spontaneous and enjoyed the act of making love.

One such month, I raised my eyebrows in an exaggerated Groucho Marx way and purred, "Ooooh, honeeeey? I'm ovulating on the left side. You wanna?"

He did, and we did.

And I got pregnant.

CHAPTER 47

Sitting in our cozy sunroom one late February afternoon, I was trying to finish the newspaper's crossword puzzle when I decided to have a beer. I had just cracked it open when I thought, *Should I be having this? What day of my cycle is it? Shouldn't I be getting my period right about now?* Distracted by these thoughts, I barely tasted the beer and then, once finished, instantly regretted my choice to drink it. I consoled myself with the knowledge that if I was pregnant, I hadn't even missed a period yet, therefore the baby wouldn't be affected.

After consulting my period-tracking calendar, I discovered that it was indeed around the time I should be getting it. Though I wasn't late yet, something must have bothered me because I told Trinity I was going to pick up a pregnancy test. He nodded absently, clearly missing the hint of stress in my voice. The next day I placed an at-home pregnancy test in my grocery cart. Then, when paying for it, I absently wondered if the cashier would judge me, as I had done as a teenager while working at White Drug. I watched her closely but saw no signs that she gave a damn. As night approached, I decided that if I hadn't gotten my period by morning, I'd take the test.

Morning arrived faster than expected and even though I was still mostly asleep it was hard to miss the bright pink box I had placed by the toilet. After rubbing my eyes and yawning a few times, I opened the box and read the directions. Ahh, man! I had to what? Pee on the tiny, thin stick? Did the makers of this pregnancy test know what an Act of God that was going to be, especially at zero dark thirty?

"Must have been designed by a man," I griped under my breath, but nevertheless I somehow managed to get the stick into my urine stream without stopping the flow or peeing on myself.

Okay, now what? The instructions say I have to wait. Really? As if this isn't stressful enough.

For sure this was designed by a man, I thought. And not only that, probably one with mother issues.

I put the pee stick on top of the box, washed my hands and left the room. *This is gonna require coffee*, I thought, so I brewed a pot. When it was finished, I poured a cup, took a sip and walked back into the bathroom.

The test showed two lines. *What does that mean? Two lines . . . two lines . . . hummm.* I searched the directions for an answer and when I found it, I thought, *Holy shit! Really!? That means I'm pregnant? Really? Yep. WHAT?! No. No, no, no, no, NO! No! I'm PREGNANT?! There has to be something wrong with this test.*

Frantically, I pawed at the box, searching for the expiration date. It showed 2013, and it was only 2011 so it wasn't outdated. *Shit.* Was the second line too faint? Did that mean I wasn't pregnant, and the test was on the fritz? I searched the instructions again but was having difficulty concentrating. Maybe I hadn't let it sit long enough. Maybe the faintness meant it was still percolating. *Yeah, that's probably it. I'll leave the room, drink some more coffee and then check again.*

I did just that and when I entered the bathroom again, the stick still showed two pink lines, one lighter than the other. *Okay, don't freak out, Melissa. There are two tests in the box, just take another one tomorrow morning. No worries.*

Oh, but I *did* worry, and the following twenty-four hours were the longest of my life. The next morning, at a slightly later hour, I repeated the procedure only to have a carbon copy of the previous test appear. What the hell?! Couldn't the test designers make this crystal clear? Did they need to leave a person wondering if they'd done something wrong? This was important shit, dammit!

With shaking hands, I showed Trinity the test.

He said, "It looks like we're pregnant."

I took great offense to that and in complete denial said, "This *fucking* test is faulty. I can't be pregnant! I ovulated on the left side."

Suggesting a blood test and saying he'd come with me, Trinity, cool as a cucumber, held my hand as we walked into the hospital. Blood was drawn and we were told a doctor would call us later that day. The day ticked by. I stared at my phone as if it were the enemy and yet was afraid to be without it.

And even after begging (and then pestering) my angels to help, it still did not ring.

Trinity came home after work and after much discussion as to who was going to call the hospital, he ended up doing it. Standing close to him, my eyes never leaving his face, I chewed off what remained of my fingernails.

"My wife was in there to have a pregnancy test this morning and we haven't heard the results. We were told someone would call us today."

Mouthing to me that they were checking, he let his gaze roam. When he regained focus I swallowed hard, knowing the person had returned to the line.

"Yes? She is? Okay, thank you. Bye."

My fingers flew out of my mouth and my neck muscles strained. *Awwww shit. Shit, shit, shit.* SHIT!

"I'm *preg*NANT?!"

He pulled me close, hugged me tightly and breathed in the smell of my hair. I clung to him and clawed at his back in order to get even closer. After a few moments, he pulled back, holding me at arm's length. Looking up, I saw a sheen of tears in his eyes.

"We're pregnant," he cooed.

Still in disbelief, my hands flew to my forehead. No. No! This couldn't be happening. I was supposed to get pregnant from the right side! Dropping my hands, I saw that Trinity's face was full of amazement. I shook my head violently and started crying.

"Noooo. No. Take it back. I'm not pregnant. Take it back!"

Pulling me into his embrace once again, he held me tightly. "Honey, honey," he soothed. "It's okay. We're fine. Breathe. Breathe."

As my tears wet his shoulder and my body shook, I mewled, "I'm so frightened, Trinity! What was I thinking?! I can't have a child at my age! Jesus, I've never been so scared. Have God take it back."

In the midst of this frenzy, I had a horrible thought, something so appalling that I couldn't say it out loud, for if I were to do so, just like my dad owning his cancer diagnosis, it might come true.

Please let me miscarry.

That thought hit me like a bucket of ice-cold water and I instantly sobered up. *What the fuck, Melissa!*

My body became pliant, and my tears stopped.

"Are you okay?" Trinity asked.

Sniffing and with eyes as big as an owls, I nodded that I was and then asked for a few minutes to myself. With one last look at me, he kissed my lips and left me where I stood.

Moving to the bedroom, I shut the door and sat on the edge of the bed where I thought about my extreme reaction. What was going on? This was everything I had wished for and yet I was paralyzed with fear.

"Help me, Guys."

Within seconds, I understood. I loved her, this life I carried, and I was mortally *terrified* of losing her. The medical community had earlier told me that due to my "advanced age" there was a fifty percent chance of miscarriage. Knowing I couldn't bear that, I said – and thought – what I did out of self-preservation.

I rested my hand on my abdomen and wiped away fresh tears. Switching my mindset from the worst-case scenario, I thought, *Baby? You've already beat the odds by implanting. Let's not stop now.*

That night, still a bit on edge even with Trinity's arms wrapped around me, I was unable to sleep and decided to review all that had gone into making this pregnancy happen. After eighteen months of trying, the baby had come to us when *she,* not us, was ready and because of that, I knew she wasn't going anywhere. Feeling that truth, I finally slept.

As we woke, still nestled together, Trinity placed a hand on my lower abdomen and asked, "How's my little girl doing?"

"She's still here, Daddy, and she's not going anywhere," I replied as I stretched and smiled.

"And how's Momma?"

"Better. So much better."

After Trinity left for work, thoughts of being pregnant, as well as why the Guys had told Susie what they did, consumed me. *They must see the bigger picture,* I concluded. *One that I'm not ready to know.*

And I was right.

CHAPTER 48

It was tough for me to believe I was pregnant because, thankfully, I didn't have any morning sickness. During the day, my increasing hormones allowed me to feel better than I had in years. At night, they granted me the sleep of the sinless. As if by osmosis, Trinity seemed to have benefited, too. Much like a proud papa, he hadn't stopped smiling since the phone call with the hospital and he continued to sleep with his hand protectively cradling my lower abdomen. Before leaving for work, he would issue orders that I should not overdo my workload and then, once there, he would text regularly to see if I had any cravings and how I was feeling.

He needn't have been concerned, though, as I knew the baby was a miracle and I wasn't about to do anything that would put either of us in the slightest bit of jeopardy. Carefully considering the changes I needed to make, I started with my lifting and cardio routine at the gym, then cut back on clients and coffee. Within weeks, my face took on a glow and a few people speculated, but they respectfully kept their silence until we were ready to break ours. We did so after the first trimester when miscarriage probabilities were drastically reduced. Until then, we kept the news between us, family and those who were like family.

Desiring a more casual and holistic birthing experience, I wanted to use a midwife. I liked the idea that they had been delivering babies for centuries. As fate would have it, one of my clients had previously delivered using a hospital midwife. Based on her glowing review, I set up an appointment.

The pregnancy finally became real when I had my first ultrasound.

"There's your peanut!" the midwife exclaimed as she nodded to the monitor.

My eyes scanned the wavy screen, but I couldn't make out anything that looked like a baby.

"Do you mean that tiny kidney bean-shaped blob thingy?" I asked.

"Exactly!" she replied. "See? Here's the head and this is what will eventually become the legs."

That's a *baby*?!

Trinity, sensing my bewilderment, squeezed my hand, letting me know he was right by my side. When I turned my head to look at him, he was wearing a silly grin and his eyes were filled with unconditional love.

I didn't know how to react or the protocol for when you are experiencing both panic and euphoria, so I opted for a forced smile. A picture of our daughter was printed and handed to me and a November due date, falling just days after Trinity's birthday, was determined.

I left the appointment feeling stupefied. After years of dreaming about being pregnant, seeing the image of the baby growing inside of me was something I couldn't fathom. But she was real even though my belly was still flat, and I had a picture to prove it. With a magnet, I displayed that proof on our fridge and then Trinity and I talked about how to tell Ian.

The next time he was with us, Trinity asked Ian if he wanted a brother or a sister someday.

"No. I like it being just me."

Trinity glanced at me and I raised my eyebrows and pursed my lips in a way that said, *Yeaaah . . . good luck with that.*

Walking to the refrigerator, Trinity removed the ultrasound picture, handed it to his eleven-year-old son and said, "What's this look like?"

Ian looked at the picture and shrugged. "I dunno."

Trinity said, "Well, what does it look like?"

"I don't know. A deer? A cow, maybe? I don't know!"

"It's a baby, Ian."

I watched the emotions play across his maturing face as he processed this. At first there was excitement; his mouth fell open, his eyes went wide, and he broke into a smile. "A baby!" he said. Then his mouth shut, and his eyes clouded over. I could tell he had realized the baby was his dad's and mine.

"You're gonna have a baby? But . . . but I wanted to stay an only child." Then, after a brief hesitation, his shoulders sagged. "Am I gonna hafta give up my bedroom?"

By this time Ian's and my relationship had vastly improved but it still fell short of what I had hoped for.

"Yes, honey," I replied. "We have to move you downstairs. The baby can't be down there in case there's a fire. You know how to get out, she can't."

Crushed, his chin fell to his chest and his gaze went to the floor. Trinity reached out and touched Ian's shoulder.

"It'll be great! What kid doesn't want a downstairs bedroom? Melissa and I think you'll really like it down there. You've got some time to get used to the idea as we don't need to move you for a while yet."

Ian mumbled a dejected okay and slowly walked towards his bedroom.

I stopped him by saying, "Should we go downstairs and plan where your bed and computer desk will go? I think we have lots of options. And don't forget, you'll also get your own bathroom but that comes with the responsibility of cleaning it."

That perked up my bonus son. By the time we had returned from the soon-to-be tweener cave, Ian was totally on board with moving, so much so that he wanted to do it immediately. Surprised and relieved, Trinity and I explained that we would need to remove the existing furniture first and suggested we wait until his next stay. Ian agreed, and when that time arrived he was still excited about setting up his new digs, where he would happily maintain camp for the next six years.

As my pregnancy progressed, a routine 3D ultrasound was scheduled. When that date arrived, Trinity was a nervous wreck, which was uncharacteristic for this unflappable war veteran. Susie and I trusted the baby was a girl, but Trinity needed reassurances that only modern technology could provide. As was the case with the healing of my precancerous cervix, medical validation was a welcomed reassurance for me as well.

The ultrasound technician spread the cold, jelly-like substance on my growing abdomen. As she moved the wand, our little girl's image flooded the computer's screen. She had grown substantially from our first view and no longer looked unrecognizable as a member of the human species. She was now the size of a melon, had legs, and was sleeping with her hands over her face and her knees tucked. Unfortunately for us, unless she moved the technician wouldn't be able to determine the sex. After doing a few yoga poses, I returned to the examining table and asked the technician to try again.

It must have worked because after a few seconds, the technician said, "I know the sex of your baby. Do you want me to write it down?"

Trinity stood and I reached for his hand as we said in unison, "NO! Tell us!"

She met our expectant gazes and without delay said, "You're having a girl."

My face broke into a beaming smile and my eyes pivoted to Trinity. Relief flickered across his face and his eyes filled with tears. Briefly closing them, he sank into the chair.

When they reopened, I said triumphantly, "I told you so. I frickin' told you so!"

His voice cracked as he said, "A girl." Then it changed to bewildered amazement. "We're having a *girrrrl!*"

But not just any girl, a *healer*; one who would help mend emotional wounds, old and new, starting with her mom and dad.

CHAPTER 49

My pregnancy was textbook; baby girl was growing at a normal rate, I was still feeling good and on track with my weight gain. While Trinity and I were making plans for the birth, we had been encouraging Ian to feel my tummy when she had the hiccups or was kicking. Each time he'd back away, wide-eyed, and shake his head no. When told that his sister might share his birthdate, he became annoyed and said that would be horrible. This troubled both of us and caused me to wonder if Ian already disliked her because she had ended his reign as an only child. In addition, I worried that he would treat her with disdain or ignore her. Even though Trinity reassured me that none of those scenarios would happen, I remained unsure.

During the last two weeks of my pregnancy I developed excruciating sciatica on my left side, which made walking very difficult. As I hobbled to my weekly midwife appointments, I often saw sympathetic gazes coming from knowing faces.

When the due date was just days away, my midwife confirmed that the baby's head was toward the birthing canal. Measurements were taken, along with the baby's heartbeat and my blood pressure, all of which confirmed that things were as they should be.

"How are you doing, Melissa?" she asked.

"I'm tired, uncomfortable and I miss being able to put on socks without being a contortionist."

She, a mother of three, said, "Once baby comes, you let go of your 'to do' list. You order food in and you eat it on paper plates that you've gotten from Amazon. You sleep whenever you can. When baby sleeps, you sleep. You do not do laundry or shower or the dishes. You do not do anything but sleep. Got it?"

I nodded and said I understood but thought, *How hard can this be? Foolish child.*

The night before her birth, I was wide awake and not happy about it. I was no longer taking clients and consoled myself with thoughts of napping the next day. As I read a book in a living room chair, Ian and Trinity slept. I noticed how quiet the house was and how active the baby had become.

What are you doing in there, baby girl? Getting ready to come out? If so, could you please do it soon, like tomorrow, so your birthday isn't the same as your brother's? He would not be very happy about that.

Much to my irritation, it was well after midnight when I finally felt tired and went to bed. Even then, sleep came in bits, and was interrupted often by the fullness of my pea-sized bladder. By morning, I was verifiably crabby and without a doubt, so over this pregnancy.

Driven by the urgency to use the bathroom for what felt like the seven hundredth time in five hours, I rolled my beached whale body out of bed. As I stood, I felt something pop and a small amount of warm fluid wet my upper legs. *Just great!* I thought as I hop-hobbled into the bathroom, turned on the light and looked down. Sure enough, my water had broken. Ungracefully, I lowered myself onto the toilet and relieved myself. When I stood, more water trickled down my legs.

Poking my head around the bathroom door, I saw that Ian was eating breakfast and Trinity was drinking coffee and reading the paper. Just another day.

Except it wasn't.

"Honey?" I said. "I think my water just broke."

The ensuing chaos was complete hilarity. Normally in control of any given situation, Trinity, his face pale, bolted from the chair and began fumbling with the newspaper. Ian stood in one spot and stared at me as if I had just grown a second head.

Then Trinity, obviously flustered, started turning in circles.

"Honey, calm down," I said. "Everything is ready and I'm not having any contractions. We're fine. Let's just call the hospital and let them know we are on our way, okay?"

Having a task seemed to help him focus because he stopped spinning and nodded his head like he had just regained his wits. While he called the hospital, Ian decided this wasn't about him and went back to eating. I showered and thought about how nice it would be to shave my legs without a baby bump in the way.

Upon our arrival at the hospital the waiting game began. I ate Oreos, my latest craving, and tried to complete the paper's crossword puzzle while Trinity watched the fetal monitor and said things like, "Get ready! This contraction's gonna be a big one!"

At first, I would smile and nod, knowing he was trying to be helpful. But then, as the unwanted notifications continued, the smiles turned into scowls. Finally, I snarled at him to knock it the hell off.

My midwife was not on call so another one attended to me. She had delivered hundreds (if not thousands) of babies during her career and while I didn't know her, I knew I was in very capable hands. Unlike my midwife, though, her manner was no-nonsense. After telling me she was going to strip my membranes in order to encourage labor, she instructed me to lie on my back, place my feet on her shoulders and relax. Not knowing the smackdown I was about to receive, I happily did as she asked, naively thinking, *If this is all labor pains are, I've got this all day long.*

Such a Pollyanna.

When the midwife started her task, searing agony ripped through my lower abdomen. I raised my head as my hands clawed into the sides of the gurney.

Is she serious?! Mother of CHRIST! *What. Is. She. Doing?!*

She didn't look up, just repeated that I should try to relax. My head returned to the table and I squeezed my eyes shut. Gritting my teeth, my mouth formed an ugly grimace. *Relax?!* My ass.

But I did try. Before she continued, I loosened my facial muscles and blew out a breath. As I did so, she took that as her cue to begin again and my body instinctively tried to stop her. A distant part of me knew she was trying to help, but I wanted her – and the excruciating torment her razor fingers brought - gone. Rising to my elbows, my hands regripped the sides of the bed. Clenching my teeth, a low growl escaped my throat as my strong legs tried to push her away. She, knowing what was coming, had already braced herself and wasn't going anywhere until she had finished lacerating my insides.

With tears streaming down my cheeks, I decided two things: I didn't like her very much and I needed to stop fighting against what she was doing.

Relaxing my legs and shaking my head as if to clear it, I said, "Oh my GOD! You've *gotta* stop!"

To my surprise, she pushed her chair backwards, took off her gloves and rose to wash her hands.

"I know that hurts, but I've got to try and speed up your delivery. This is the first step. If you don't start to have contractions that are coming closer together, we'll give you Pitocin. That'll make your contractions stronger and will help move the baby into the birthing canal."

Then she opened a cupboard, removed something and sat it on the counter. "You're going to bleed a bit. Here's some pads." And with that, she exited the room, and left me uncharacteristically speechless.

CHAPTER 50

After several hours, the contractions had still not accelerated. But once Pitocin was introduced, they deepened, taking my breath away and causing tears to bloom. The nurses reminded me to breathe, saying things like, "If you don't breathe, your baby can't breathe," while Trinity sat on the edge of a chair watching the fetal monitor again. This time, when large contractions were indicated, he'd look away guiltily. Exasperated, I asked a nurse to turn the screen away from us. Sending a knowing glance in Trinity's direction, she did as I asked.

By this time my husband was Reiki One trained, so I asked him to give me some energy. Flexing his fingers as if they needed limbering, he lightly placed them on my upper back and arm. His timing couldn't have been worse; another hard contraction had begun, and I didn't want to be touched.

"Eew. God no." I snapped, shaking his hands off. "Don't touch me. Just send me energy from your chair."

Seeing how my abruptness had hurt his feelings, after the contraction passed, I said, "Honey. I'm sorry. I just can't be touched right now. I don't know why, maybe it's because of the pain. Can you just intend for the energy to go to me, please?"

He nodded and aimed his hands towards me.

Throughout my pregnancy, I had been "banking" Reiki, saving energy for the future knowing that I would need it during the delivery process. Now, as I was gripped by a strong contraction, I mentally asked for some of that energy to be delivered. Immediately, as if I had received an epidural, the pain decreased, and the effects lasted about fifteen minutes, giving me an appreciated break.

One of the nurses had suggested that I use a birthing ball if the pain in my lower back became too intense. When she brought it in, I looked at her suspiciously because it was nothing more than a plain old exercise ball, the kind I had used hundreds of times at the gym. And while I was very comfortable using them there, I soon discovered it was a whole new ballgame doing so when nine months pregnant. As the energetic analgesic wore off, I became restless and thought the "birthing" ball might help.

Since I hadn't asked how to utilize it for pain reduction, I decided to start by sitting on it. Trinity and I timed it so there was enough of a break between the end of one contraction and the start of another. He helped me out of bed, then kept the tangle of cords from tripping me as I waddled to the ball.

With his hands holding my upper body, supporting me, I attempted to lower myself onto the ball. Splaying my legs to steady myself, I took a deep breath and closed my eyes as the next contraction hit. Once it passed, Trinity, still standing next to me, asked if everything was good. I opened my eyes, smiled and said yes, at which point he dropped the cords, touched my shoulder and walked to the window. He was looking out it when I rolled off the ball.

Startled, I flung my arms wide and looked frantically for something to stop my fall. Finding nothing, with a whoosh, I landed flat on my back and then started giggling because that could only happen to me. I heard the intake of Trinity's breath as warm liquid saturated my upper thighs and lower back.

Trinity rounded the bed's corner, looking frightened.

"I'm okay!" I said before he could ask, then I added sheepishly, "I *clearly* don't have the balance I thought I had."

I paused for a breath. "Honey, umm. I think I peed myself or I'm hemorrhaging." Then, giggling, "God, this pregnancy stuff is so glamorous."

He looked and said there wasn't any blood, but he was going to get the nurse anyway.

I stopped him in mid-stride. "Dude. Can you help me up first, please?"

A nurse entered the room as he was doing so. Seeing us struggle, her eyes went from the spreading wetness to the birthing ball. "What happened?!"

"Oh, I fell off the ball. I'm fine but I think I emptied my bladder and I'm kind of embarrassed about that."

After she assisted Trinity, I limped to the bathroom intent on cleaning myself. Once there, I felt an all too familiar urge. *This is ridiculous!* I thought. *I just went potty!* Sighing, I resigned myself to the task at hand and while doing so, asked God to *please* let me finish before another contraction began. Surprised by the steady flow, I forgot my social skills and blurted, "Hey, you guys? I'm peeing again and it's a lot, so if I didn't pee myself and it's not blood, what is it?"

The nurse said my front water broke. Before I could answer, another contraction hit.

"What?" I asked once it had passed. "Front water?"

As she helped me back to bed, she explained that sometimes as the baby moves lower, the amniotic sac gets squished, causing fluid to remain. Once I was settled, she checked our vitals, and then for crowning. It was then that her face changed; she didn't like what she had felt. Removing her gloves, she prodded and poked my tummy. I watched as her eyes went to the ceiling, processing the information. When she reached a conclusion, she excused herself and returned moments later with another nurse.

The second nurse's face wore a look of concern. Without any small talk, she began touching my tummy, pressing hard in a few places, then, after checking for crowning, she gave a curt, closed-lip nod to the other nurse and said they'd be right back. As they left, my questioning eyes found Trinity's. When the nurses returned, the membrane-stripping midwife was with them.

Awwww shit.

CHAPTER 51

When the trio entered, I had been composing a text to update my family. This immediately took a backseat to the midwife's face. Without saying a word, she repeated the nurse's actions and even though she didn't give anything away, I wasn't fooled. I knew something was wrong.

Confirming that, she stood back and said, "Your baby is breach. We have to do a C-section immediately."

"No way," I protested. "I want a vaginal birth. It's all I've prepared for. Can't you turn her around?"

"No. We don't do that anymore. It's too dangerous. Besides, we don't have time for this. We need to get you to surgery right now before the baby advances any further into the birthing canal. Every minute matters now. I need to remind you not to push. We are going to have you sign some forms and insert a catheter and an IV line."

Undaunted, I tried again. "But . . . but, I *want* to give birth vaginally. Isn't there anything we can do?"

Sympathetic, but undeterred, she said, "No. You are at risk and so is your baby. I've seen this many times and you need to be prepped for surgery immediately. This is the only option."

With those words, fingers of panic cut through my confidence. Knowing she wouldn't budge, and that I was unwilling to jeopardize our lives, I lowered my eyes, swallowed hard and nodded my approval.

I looked for my husband as tears of frustration filled my eyes. Goddammit! I wanted a normal birth, not a C-section, and I wanted to do it without an epidural, as I had envisioned. Fearing a longer recovery time, I didn't want surgery in addition to giving birth and breastfeeding because at forty-six, despite wanting to believe the opposite, I wouldn't bounce back as I would have in my twenties or thirties.

As I was trying to cope with the feelings of powerlessness, two employees, one male and one female, entered my now chaotic room. Standing a few feet from the bed, they talked about who was going to insert the IV. I heard the male nervously ask, "Do you think I'm ready?" to which the presumably more experienced woman said it was up to him.

The dialogue continued for almost a minute when I'd had enough. Unwilling to be anyone's guinea pig and feeling as if they were unaware of me, I whisper-yelled, a la Rya, "Hey! You!"

The woman raised her head first, but with a rather disoriented expression that only added to my stress.

Pointing at her, I said, "You are going to insert the IV. I've had enough pain for one day and this day's not over yet."

Jesus. Really?

Remembering the unfinished text message, I picked up my phone intent on completing it when the midwife's voice rang out, "Dad, you'll be outfitted with a sterile suit so you can be in the operating room with her. Mom, we need to move you *now*."

Judging by her tone, I knew there wouldn't be any time to say what I had wanted to say. Instead, thinking that some news was better than none, I pressed send and immediately regretted that decision. Knowing this *could* be my last correspondence, I wanted to tell those precious few that I loved them. *Oh well. They know*, I thought, and then I threw the phone to my stunned husband.

As the bed started to move, I took in his handsome face. On it was a level of anxiety and worry that I had never witnessed. He was nervously licking his lips as his eyes darted around the room taking in the scene. Standing apart from the fray, he looked vulnerable and I wondered how he was doing and who would comfort him during my absence.

Frightened, I hastily said a prayer, *Please God, don't take me away from him. Not yet. Not now. I love him so much. But know this, if it comes down to my life or the baby's, then take mine. You got that? My life for hers, no question.*

As the bed was being pushed into the hallway, our eyes locked and with one hand protecting my bulging abdomen, I reached for him with the other. He lunged for it, but the distance was too great; only our fingertips touched. Then the bed and all its surrounding commotion completed its departure, leaving him alone and in silence.

Needing him to hear it as much as I needed to say it, I shouted, "I love you!"

"I love you, too! I'll be with you in a few minutes!"

Away from him, panic turned into fear and I channeled that into anger. *What are You doing, God!? You know I wanted to give birth vaginally, so why is this happening? I'm so fuckin' pissed at You right now. I feel so betrayed. Why are You allowing this to happen?!*

Within hours, I would learn the answer.

CHAPTER 52

The environment of the operating room was harsh and sterile, a far cry from the inviting, warmly lit birthing room I had left. Trinity, dressed in a white hygienic body suit with only his face visible, waited for me. *God?* I thought, my anger resurfacing, *This is not the way I wanted to bring my daughter into the world!*

As two strong men were about to lift me off the hospital bed and onto the operating table, another contraction left me clutching the sheets and breathing through clenched teeth. *Fucking Pitocin is evil,* I thought and then asked if they could give me a moment. Looking to – and receiving – approval from whomever was in charge, they put me down, and with wide eyes, backed away from my writhing body. As the pain subsided, I said I was ready. They returned and on the count of three lifted me up, gently laid me on the operating table, and then helped me into a seated position.

Having previously visited with me about what would occur, the anesthesiologist got right to work. Another contraction was coming so I motioned for her to hold off. During it, she reminded me to breathe and told me not to push. I wanted to tell her, in a not-so-nice manner that I knew that, but instead I nodded and once it had passed, she inserted the needle.

"It'll take a few moments," she said, "but then you shouldn't be able to feel your legs."

After a few moments, I said, "Umm . . . I can still feel my legs."

"Are you joking?"

Oh lady, if you only knew that most of my personality abandoned me early this morning while my feet were on a midwife's shoulders.

"No, I'm not kidding. I can still feel my legs."

And then, as if to prove my point, I felt the start of another contraction. "Shit," I panted. "Wait. I'm having another contraction." I tried to double over but the basketball-sized baby living in my abdomen made that impossible. Breathing through it, I told her to have another go and this time the needle found its mark. Blissfully, it was buh-bye contractions.

I was then helped into a supine position and my arms were laid out on wooden slats. I thought I looked a bit like Jesus on the cross. Sitting at my head, a guy told me he was going to monitor my vitals and keep me happy.

"Keep me happy?" I asked.

"Yeah. I'm the morphine man."

Laughing, I told him I appreciated his sense of humor.

The surgeon and a nurse entered the room and, judging by their conversation about grown children and recent vacations, I could tell they were old friends. What seemed like a few minutes later, the doctor stepped back from my abdomen and said, "You have some really strong abs."

Uhhh, thanks? Because I was not able to see what she was doing, I pivoted my head to my husband, who shrugged his shoulders. I then guessed that the procedure had started, and she was slicing her way into my womb.

Their banter continued and Mr. Morphine Man kept his drug and personality coming. Having nothing to do but wait, I thought about how angry and frustrated I was and when tears seeped from my eyes and rolled into my hair, Trinity touched my arm and asked if I was okay. Not ready to share my thoughts, I simply nodded.

After the morphine dude asked how I was doing, the surgeon said, "Well! Will you look at that? See? Right here? This would be a great teaching experience for someone."

"Ooooooh. Uh huh, yessss," came the nurses drawn-out reply.

With amazement, the surgeon asked her, "Have you ever seen anything like this?"

The nurse replied she hadn't and before I could say anything, the doctor assured me I was doing fine and then asked if I knew I had a bicornuate uterus.

"A what?"

"It's where the uterus is split in two."

"Uhhhh nope. I didn't know."

A moment later, lifting my daughter into the air and swinging her towards me, she said, "Here's your little girl! She's looking good so far."

Into my line of vision floated an obviously annoyed baby. Her body was still in the fetal position and a large portion of the umbilical cord was wrapped around her neck. Her clenched fists waved in the air and her beautiful face wore an indignant expression. When her dark eyes met mine, I couldn't help but laugh. *I know, baby girl. I know. This wasn't the way I wanted to do this, but we are rolling with it.* Then, as quickly as she was brought into view, she was retracted. My eyes filled with tears and I thought it was cruel to take my daughter out of my sight after I had waited a lifetime to see her.

Telling Trinity it was time for him to leave and go be with our daughter, the surgeon told me I was doing well, and that she would stitch me up and get me to my baby girl as soon as possible. Thanking her, I told Mr. Morphine Personality Man that I was itchy. He said that was a side effect and that he'd give me something to make it stop.

"Hurry," I said, and then I slept.

CHAPTER 53

During the pregnancy, we had been entertaining the names of Jessie, Athena, Brigga and Paris, but none of them seemed to fit. Then, one night in my third trimester, five names came to me as I slept. Rousing myself long enough to write them on a bedside notepad, I shared them with Trinity the next morning.

"I dreamt five names last night, honey. They were Jarin, Deep, Tesha, Sentra and Ceta. I think Jarin and Deep are for a boy, but I like the others. How about you?"

"Sentra is a car and I dated a Tessa so Tesha won't work."

I raised an eyebrow and said, "Dated? You mean slept with?"

He shrugged and flashed me a devil-may-care smile.

Shaking my head, I said, "Good Lord. If we're gonna eliminate the names of every girl you 'dated,' we're in trouble."

"I like Ceta," he said, "but there can't be an 'h' at the end of it. I've never understood why people put a silent letter at the end of a name. It's confusing and so not necessary."

Nodding, I said, "I really like Ceta, too. It's unique. Can we have her middle name be Jessie after my grandma?"

He nodded and said we could. Over the next few weeks, we tried out that name, as well as a few others, but kept returning to it.

I awoke to a darkened room where the only light came from behind a nearly-closed bathroom door. Using that, I looked for Trinity and found him sleeping in an awkward position on a small, fold-out bed.

For the millionth time, I was envious of his ability to sleep whenever and wherever, something he had learned in the Gulf War.

Except for the hiss of an air machine that was filling the bubble wrap-like material around my legs, all was quiet.

Just past my toes, sleeping in a clear bassinet, was our daughter. She looked so tiny and my heart swelled with love. Needing to hold her, I tried to move my legs, but they wouldn't respond. Not letting that stop me, I pushed myself into a seated position where I intended to manually move my legs.

Hearing the rustling sheets and creaking bed, Trinity awoke. In a voice that sounded like he had smoked a carton of cigarettes, he said, "Hi honey. How ya doin'?"

He was disheveled, bleary-eyed and looked both vulnerable and boyish. It was a look I had always loved.

"I'm fine," I said. "There's no pain, but I want to see our baby."

Rising, he walked to the bassinette, scooped her up and brought her to me.

Swaddled in a standard hospital-issued cotton blanket, she wore a hat which the nurses had customized with a bow. Seeing how tiny she looked in her daddy's big hands caused my eyes to fill with tears. Reaching for her, Trinity placed her in my arms, and I brought her to my chest. While cradling and rocking her from side to side, I said, "Hi, baby. Hi. Welcome to the world. I'm your mommy and this guy is your daddy. You've got a brother, too, but he's not here right now. We've been waiting for you. It's so nice to finally hold you."

As if sensing me, she opened her eyes and with a look that was both attentive and curious, studied my face. Feeling the caress of her gaze, the welling tears overflowed and streamed down my cheeks. Marveling at how, just hours before she had been inside me and now I was holding her, came an unsettling thought, *I can't keep her safe and protected anymore and this world is so messed up.*

Just then, the seasoned midwife entered the room after a soft knock. Checking my chart, she asked how I was doing and if I was in any pain. When I told her that I was fine and there wasn't any pain, she nodded.

All of a sudden, I remembered what the surgeon had told me during the C-section, and I asked her if she would explain what a deviated uterus was.

"Sure," she said and then drew a picture that showed a normal, pear shaped organ. After showing it to us, she then drew a line dividing the drawing into two unequal parts.

"Your little girl implanted on the left side, which was a good thing because that's the larger of the two sections. If she would have implanted on the significantly smaller side, there's a good chance you would have miscarried, and possibly died. The other good thing is that the baby was small, because if she was bigger, neither of you may have survived."

You could have heard a pin drop. My staring eyes looked at Trinity whose mouth had fallen open. *Oh. My. GOD!*

As if that wasn't enough, she continued. "It's very common for babies in this type of deviated – or bicornuate - environment to be born breech because once they get bigger, they are unable to turn. Lastly, if she would have been born vaginally, there was a high chance she would have been strangled by the umbilical cord. Luckily, none of that happened, and Mom and baby are doing just fine. Any questions?"

Uh no. That about does it, I think.

Stunned, we both shook our heads and with that, she offered a smile and left as quietly as she had entered.

The magnitude of her words overwhelmed both of us and caused my unblinking eyes to fill with tears yet again. Glancing at Trinity and then at our sleeping newborn, the knowledge I had been seeking, and sometimes demanding, finally materialized.

I understood everything, and when Trinity rose from his seat and stood next to me, I knew he did too.

Reaching for his hand, I looked at the precious miracle laying on my chest. Finally blinking, tears cascaded unchecked down my cheeks, neck and then rolled into my hospital gown.

"Oh my God, Trinity. OH. MY. GOD!"

His hand squeezed mine, causing me to look at him and notice his cheeks were tear-stained too.

I said, "Thank God He put this midwife in our path, Trinity. Thank God! I don't even wanna think what might have happened if she hadn't been here. I was so resentful and so *angry* with Him for not letting me deliver naturally and all He was doing was saving our lives." The tears then turned into sobs as I continued, "I feel like a complete ass."

Trinity kissed my forehead and let his lips linger before taking a page out of my book. "Everything happens for a reason, you know," he murmured. "There are no coincidences."

Then, still holding my hand, he reached to caress our six-pound, six-ounce bundle, and the three of us became one.

CHAPTER 54

The next morning, after the surgeon had checked both my incision and chart, she asked if I was in any pain. When I replied that I wasn't, her surprised blue eyes connected with mine, allowing me an unsolicited glimpse of her spiritual beauty that hit me like a lightning bolt.

"It shows here the last time you've had morphine was last night," she said, "and you declined ibuprofen this morning. Are you sure you're not in any pain?"

Captivated by the astral colors swirling around her, I barely heard the question. Instead, my eyes roamed, taking in her brilliance and thinking she was the perfect soul to bring our daughter into this world.

Her inquiry hung in the air until I realized that I had been staring. Then, having received the remaining stored Reiki during the night, I flashed her a grin and answered with a quiet shake of my head.

ABOUT THE AUTHOR

Melissa Schaff is an intuitive, medium, Reiki Master and author who writes about her personal experiences with intuition, angels, the afterlife and her overly stubborn husband.

After leaving behind a twenty-one-year banking career, Melissa was called to combine all three of her childhood occupational choices - acting, psychology, and nursing - into one perfectly blended role. Having also experienced firsthand the healing powers of Reiki, she began her training and eventually became a Reiki Master Practitioner. Today, she owns Inner Focus Reiki, where she uniquely weaves her wit, intuitive gifts and wisdom to help empower, inspire and enlighten all who find her.

Melissa strongly supports veterans, recovering alcoholics/addicts and is available for Intuitive Reiki, group sessions, public speaking, and media appearances. She lives with her family in Fargo, North Dakota.

To find out more about Melissa or her latest offerings, connect with her at www.InnerFocusReiki.com or Facebook @MelissaSchaffAuthor.

9 781733 277389